ALCOHOLISM'S CHILDREN

ALCOHOLISM'S CHILDREN

ACoAs in priesthood and religious life

SEAN SAMMON, FMS

ALBA · HOUSE   NEW · YORK

SOCIETY OF ST. PAUL, 2187 VICTORY BLVD., STATEN ISLAND, NEW YORK 10314

155.94
SaS

Library of Congress Cataloging-in-Publication Data

Sammon, Sean D., 1947 -
  Alcoholism's Children: ACoAs in priesthood
 and religious life / Sean D. Sammon.
    p.   cm.
   1. Adult children of alcoholics. 2. Alcoholics —
Family relationships. 3. Catholic Church — Clergy.
I. Title.
    ISBN 0-8189-0545-X
    HV5132.S25   1989   88-39524
    362.2'92 — dc19   CIP

Designed, printed and bound in the United States of
America by the Fathers and Brothers of the
Society of St. Paul, 2187 Victory Boulevard,
Staten Island, New York 10314, as part of their
communications apostolate.

Printing Information:

Current Printing - first digit 1 2 3 4 5 6 7 8 9 10 11 12

Year of Current Printing - first year shown
1989 1990 1991 1992 1993 1994 1995 1996

DEDICATION

With thanks
to

Craig F. Evans,
a
treasured friend
of almost
a quarter century

CONTENTS

INTRODUCTION

APPROXIMATELY 28 million Americans have at least one alcoholic parent. Most children of alcoholics (CoAs) remain invisible; they seek approval; their coping behavior is socially acceptable. A disproportionate number, however, also enter the criminal justice system, courts, prisons, mental health facilities, Employee Assistance Programs, and are referred to school authorities.

What are some of the facts about CoAs? First of all, they are prone to suffer a range of somatic illnesses and psychological disturbances: compulsive achieving, eating disorders, learning disabilities, anxiety, depression, and suicide attempts. Second, CoAs usually experience spiritual problems: emptiness, a lack of purpose in life, the false hope that a miracle will bring some relief. Third, at high risk to develop the disease of alcoholism, children of alcoholics are frequent victims of child neglect, incest, and other forms of family violence and exploitation and often marry someone who becomes addicted. At least half the women who marry alcoholic men were raised in homes

where one or more family members were chemically
dependent.

Alcoholism is a family affair. Every member suffers its effects. In time, all become as sick as the addicted person. Priests and men and women religious,
for example, who grew up with chemically dependent
parents can remember their family's pain. In later
years many realize that entering the minor seminary or
juniorate gave them some distance from the problems
at home. One woman's admission to religious life freed
her from the sexual advances of her intoxicated father.
Likewise, the unpredictable anger of a young man's
mother concerned him less after he entered the minor
seminary. Only as an adult did he understand the
connection between her rages and her alcoholism.

CoAs adapt to the chaos and inconsistency in their
families by denying their feelings. Many also develop
these characteristics: an inability to trust, an over-
developed sense of responsibility, an addiction to ex-
citement, and fears of abandonment, conflict, loss of
control. What are the results? Isolation, low self-
esteem, difficulty maintaining satisfying relationships,
depression, guilt, and shame.

Until recently most people gave little thought to
men and women who grew up in chemically dependent families. Why worry? Weren't a number of them
successful and outstanding members of their profes-
sions? Apparently unscarred from their family experience, they were referred to as "invulnerable" children.
Of course, some CoAs had problems later in life, but,
in general, concern about their physical, emotional,
and spiritual health and their relationships with others

was limited. Instead, attention focused on the chemically dependent person.

This book is written for adult children of alcoholics (ACoAs) and those who know and care about them. It is a simple and straightforward explanation of the difficulties ACoAs face and what they must do to recover. While addressed to all ACoAs the book pays particular attention to those who are priests and men and women religious. Both life choices provide a framework where ACoAs may live out the debilitating patterns of behavior learned during their formative years in the family.

The text is divided into three parts. The first includes a chapter that defines the disease of alcoholism, discusses its progression, and examines the defenses used by many addicted men and women.

Part Two is made up of two chapters. The first describes addicted families as systems that have lost their balance and examines their rules. The second discusses the roles taken on by the members of these families in their attempts to adjust to the alcoholism in their midst.

Finally, the first of Part Three's two chapters answers this question: what do ACoAs need to do to recover and what resources are available to help? The second suggests steps people can take when intervening in the life of a chemically dependent person.

Reflection questions are included at the end of each chapter. They will help you think about what you have read, internalize any thoughts you find helpful, and, if you are the child of an alcoholic, make decisions about what steps you need to take in your own recovery.

This book does not exhaust discussion about alcoholism or its children; rather, it tells briefly the story of a potentially fatal disease that affects millions of Americans and their families. The text also points out that, today, recovery from alcoholism and its legacy is possible, perhaps more so than ever before. If you are a child from an alcoholic family, I hope that reading this book will convince you of the wisdom of this paradox: the disease that you once thought might take your life can be the very thing that makes it worth living.

A few clarifications will make your reading easier. First of all, the terms alcoholism, addiction, and chemical and drug dependency are all used in this book to refer solely to the disease of alcoholism and the alcoholic man or woman. Second, the phrase children of alcoholics (CoAs) is not age specific; it includes anyone growing up in an alcoholic family. The term adult children of alcoholics (ACoAs), however, is more restricted and refers to *adult* men and women with at least one alcoholic parent. Third, if you wish to learn more about any topic discussed in the text, references are provided at the end of each chapter; they should give you the information you seek.

Writing a book is never a solitary venture. This effort was no exception. A word of thanks to several people who read the text as it was in the making and offered helpful suggestions: Craig F. Evans, Kathleen E. Kelley, John E. Kerrigan, Jr., Marie Kraus, S.N.D., John Malich, F.M.S., John Mulligan, F.M.S., John P.

Nash, F.M.S., and Hank Sammon, F.M.S. If this book is clear, easy to read, and consistent, they deserve the credit. They should not, however, be held responsible for its conclusions.

A special word of thanks to my editor at Alba House, Rev. Anthony Chenevey, S.S.P. He is a very patient man. This book should have been finished several months ago but was delayed because of new responsibilities that I took up in June 1987 as a provincial in my congregation, the Marist Brothers of the Schools. I can still hear Father Chenevey's encouraging voice on the phone as I missed deadline after deadline. He provided a positive and hopeful spirit when I wondered if this text would ever see the light of day.

The book is dedicated to Craig F. Evans, a treasured friend of almost a quarter century. Having worked for a number of years in the addiction field, he really should have written it. Craig first sparked my interest in the topic of alcoholism; he is a valued colleague and has always been a source of professional growth for me. More importantly, though, he has taught me a great deal about the meaning of friendship and for that I am very grateful.

SEAN D. SAMMON, F.M.S.
Watertown, Massachusetts
10 July 1988

PART I

ALCOHOLISM

CHAPTER I

The Disease Of Alcoholism

Jeff was annoyed. His friend Susan had just left; while they were at lunch, she expressed her concern about this 44-year-old religious brother's drinking. "I don't drink any more than others in my community," thought Jeff. "Sure, I look forward to a drink or two before supper to help me relax; maybe I also like a few beers or some wine with the meal and later in the evening, but so do a lot of other people." "Susan's just uptight," Jeff thought to himself. "Why, the restaurant she picked out today didn't even have a bar! No, I don't have a drinking problem."

In recent months, however, a number of the men in Jeff's community have also become concerned about his drinking. Joe, for example, noticed that Jeff often continued drinking after most of the community was in bed. A few times he was so intoxicated Joe had to help him to his room.

There was also the occasion two months ago when Jeff had been drinking and was in a really ugly mood during a community party. He was just plain nasty to Joe. The next day, however, Jeff had no recollection of their argument.

Fred noticed that Jeff appeared more and more preoccupied with alcohol. He had established a ritual around having a drink before dinner. His "drink," though, was about twice the size of anyone else's. Sometimes Jeff had two or three and got terrible if anything interferred with this pattern. Fred knew that Jeff prided himself on his ability to "hold his liquor"; when other people called it quits, he would often continue drinking with little apparent effect. Jeff reported that his father was much the same in this regard.

ALCOHOLISM is a chronic, progressive, life-threatening disease with no known cure. It affects people's physical, emotional, spiritual, and mental well-being and their ability to make choices. The disease can be arrested and treated, but abstinence is only the first step on the road to sobriety.

The authors of *The Harvard Medical School Mental Health Letter* compare alcoholism to high blood pressure. The two conditions share a number of similarities. Both cause physical damage; heredity, social condition, and a person's attitude and emotional state affect each of them. The specific causes of high blood pressure and alcoholism are also unknown and the line separating the normal from the abnormal is not always clear. What is the best treatment for both conditions? A change in behavior.

The American Medical Association gave formal recognition to the disease concept of alcoholism in 1956. Many people, however, still think of it as a vice and addicted men and women as weak-willed individuals who care little about others or themselves. Unfortunately, many chemically dependent people are among the last to accept the disease concept.

Psychiatrist George Vaillant estimates that alcoholism will afflict between three and ten percent of all Americans at some time during their lives. It is no respecter of age, sex, creed, or race.

The annual medical and social costs of alcoholism exceed the bill for cancer and respiratory disease combined. In the United States alone, the disease is involved in at least a quarter of all admissions to general hospitals, and plays a major role in the most common causes of death among men ages twenty to forty: suicide, homicide, and accidents. Later in life, it contributes to cancer, cirrhosis of the liver, and other chronic illnesses.

The disease's damage is not limited to those afflicted: one in every three U.S. families reports alcohol abuse by a member. The drug is a significant factor in up to 90% of child abuse cases. Former First Lady Betty Ford points out that prenatal exposure to high levels of chemicals can cause death through spontaneous abortion or stillbirth and lead to malformation, retardation, and growth deficiency. This alcohol fetal syndrome is the third leading cause of birth defects in the United States. Acoholism and its effects are national problems.

Difficult Diagnosis

There is no easy way to diagnose alcoholism and the disease's image must not be oversimplified or exaggerated. No single symptom is decisive, not even high alcohol consumption. Many people mistakenly confuse the chemically dependent person with the stereotypic skid-row drunk. Only three percent of all alcoholic men and women fall into this category. Many addicted persons never experience withdrawal symptoms; most hold jobs and sustain a family or community life for a long time.

Each addicted person is different and questions such as, "Do I have a drinking problem?" and, "Am I an alcoholic?" lack ready answers. For example, neither the quantity of alcohol consumed nor a person's ability to stop drinking is an accurate measure of addiction. One or two drinks per day pose no difficulty for one person; a glass of wine is a serious problem for another. Many actively alcoholic men and women can point to weeks, months, and even years of abstinence.

Other facts cloud the diagnostic picture. Factors that would help detect high-risk drinkers are elusive; drinking patterns vary. Addicted men and women are not always drinking. Some imbibe only on weekends or restrict their drinking to certain hours of the day or days of the week; others drink throughout the day. How, then, can people tell if they are alcoholic?

Answers Differ

Dennis Wholey, host of the PBS television series *Late Night America* and a recovering alcoholic, offers this simple test of the disease. Starting today, set a reasonable limit on the number of drinks you will consume each day for the next ninety days. The number doesn't matter — two, three, even four drinks daily — so long as it is reasonable. Regardless of what happens during the next ninety days, agree to stay with that number. No excuses for graduations, anniversary celebrations, promotions or difficulties at work. If you exceed the agreed-upon number, you have a drinking problem.

Researchers at Johns Hopkins University Hospital answered the question differently, developing a twenty-item questionnaire to measure alcohol addiction. The test examines the effects of alcohol on work, family life, relationships, self-esteem, and sleep. People are asked if they crave a drink at a definite time each day, eat irregularly or not at all while drinking, are sometimes uncomfortable if alcohol is not available, drink alone or in the morning, resent the advice of those who try to get them to stop drinking, or drink to escape worries and troubles. (See Appendix A for an example of an alcohol addiction questionnaire.)

Other definitions exist. Psychotherapist Brother John Mulligan, F.M.S., describes alcoholism as the continued compulsive use of the drug in the face of adverse consequences. If people's use of alcohol causes *any* continuing disruption in their personal, physical, social, spiritual, or economic life and they *do not terminate its use, that* constitutes harmful dependence.

Nonalcoholic people might have family problems over *one* drinking episode, *one* reprimand from an employer, *one* brush with the law. Any of these events is enough to cause them to say: "If drinking leads to this kind of trouble, I'm going to cut this stuff out." They do just that. Alcoholic men and women, however, continue drinking, even though it gives rise to ongoing problems in any or all of their important relationships. Addicted persons adapt their lifestyle to the use of the chemical; they do not change their use so as not to interfere with the demands of that lifestyle. By the late stages of the disease, alcohol has become progressively the most important thing in the chemically dependent person's life.

What is the best predictor of alcoholism? A family history of addiction. Alcoholism runs in families; it is a generational disease. Claudia Black, drawing on extensive pioneering work with children of alcoholics, estimates conservatively that fifty to sixty percent of all alcoholic persons have, or had, at least one chemically dependent parent. Other researchers report that boys with an alcoholic parent are five times more likely to develop the disease than boys from families with many problems but no alcoholic parent. The results of still other investigations estimate that the biological sons of alcoholic men have four times the average rate of alcoholism, even those raised by nonalcoholic adoptive parents. Genetics and environment both appear to play a role in the onset and progression of the disease.

Progression Of The Disease

Most drinking starts as social drinking. Many adolescents, experimenting with alcohol, discover that the drug changes the way they feel. On occasion, some of them drink too much due to insecurity or social pressure. Eventually, they learn about alcohol's effects and develop a pattern of use.

Alcohol therapist Sharon Wegscheider points out that for most people early learning about the effects of alcohol marks the beginning of a lifetime pattern of social drinking. Unfortunately, for every ten to fifteen experimenting teenagers who can look forward to the uneventful enjoyment of alcoholic beverages, at least one other has taken the first step toward alcohol dependency.

Alcoholism's Early Days

Alcoholism's early days are often neither dramatic nor memorable. One religious sister's addiction began with a friend's suggestion that a glass of wine at bedtime would help her insomnia.

A diocesan priest initiated his dependency by drinking alone at the end of the day. In time, he resented late-night phone calls or the doorbell's ring when they interrupted his ritual with alcohol.

Early in the disease process alcoholic persons develop a *preoccupation with the drug*. They think and talk about it; they look forward to drinking and anticipate the feeling the drug gives them. At social gatherings, they wonder if alcohol will be served and, when dining out, give priority to restaurants where liquor is available. Alcohol also anesthetizes some of the addicted person's feelings; the drug helps them avoid facing them. In time, alcoholic men and women develop a *primary relationship* with the drug: they become more interested in drinking than in being with the people they love.

Normal drinkers do not share these concerns. Even if they get intoxicated at a family get-together or on New Year's Eve, the nonaddicted person lacks the preoccupation with alcohol which clearly marks the chemically dependent person.

Warning Signs

1. Increased Tolerance

An acquired increased tolerance for alcohol is an early warning sign that heavy social drinking is moving toward trouble. People find they need more and more of the drug to achieve the desired effect. Where two drinks once sufficed, three or four are needed now to reach the same euphoric state; a relaxing cocktail before dinner begins to appear every night instead of just on Fridays. An ability to "drink everyone else under the table" is not proof that some people can handle their alcohol better than others; instead, it is an indication of a growing tolerance not found usually in nonalcoholic people. With increased usage comes deeper and deeper shame, guilt, and remorse. One paradoxical fact to keep in mind: as the alcoholic man or woman ages, tolerance for the drug usually begins to decline.

2. Blackouts

Blackouts also signal a problem with alcohol. These chemically induced amnesias often occur with the heavy use of the drug. They should not be confused with "passing out," the total loss of consciousness. During a blackout people may function in an otherwise normal fashion; however, they experience complete memory loss for a period of time. Later they are unable to recall anything about the blackout period and they never will.

About two-thirds of all alcoholic men and women, and some nonaddicted drinkers, report blackouts. These episodes increase in frequency and duration as alcohol abuse continues, and can eventually last an evening or longer. They also become more unpredictable. Blackouts sometimes continue to occur even after the alcoholic person stops drinking.

During a blackout, people sometimes do not appear very intoxicated; those around them assume that they are in control of their faculties. Their memory, however, fails to function: they can't remember what they did while under the influence. For example, an evening's conversation goes unrecorded; promises and commitments are not retained; some people don't remember driving home or how they got to bed; many repeat themselves: they tell the same story or joke over several times.

Friends, family and community members, and co-workers frequently stumble upon the alcoholic person's blackouts when a promise goes unkept. An intoxicated religious teaching brother, for example, agreed to attend a Saturday-morning meeting to work on the following school year's class schedule but, having no recollection of his earlier promise, went instead with a colleague to watch the high-school football team's workout.

In another example, a friend's reminder saved a married middle-aged woman from the embarrassment of "forgetting" that during a recent party she had invited a colleague to dinner. This woman, having blacked out, had no recollection about extending the invitation. Finally, a parish priest, perplexed by a parishioner's coolness, failed to recall his own insulting comments made in a recent phone conversation during an evening's drinking.

While researchers disagree about the point at which a person crosses the threshold from social drinking to alcohol abuse, many suggest that blackouts provide certain evidence of the drinker's addiction.

As the disease develops, the length of blackouts increases. Wegscheider provides the unusually dramatic example of a man sent to a treatment center by his employer when his alcoholism began affecting his work. He asked for information about hospital alcohol treatment units and left, presumably to be admitted to one.

A few weeks later, however, the man returned to the center and requested the same information. Blacked out for two to three weeks, he was unaware of his previous visit. The man's last memory was of leaving home one morning to seek help for his disease. He had no idea when that was or where he had been since. Only later, when his credit card bills arrived in the mail, did he learn that he had been all over the country, staying in motels, running up bills, and doing he knew not what else. One of the terrors of a blackout is this "not knowing."

Alcoholic men and women experience considerable fear, bewilderment, and depression as a result of their blackouts. They begin to wonder: "What did I do last night after nine o'clock?" "Who was I with?" "Where did I leave the car?" Their anxiety, however, leads them to minimize or discredit any firsthand accounts of their behavior while blacked out; they think people are exaggerating. In time, many addicted people come to believe that others are unfairly criticizing their chemical use.

As these and other symptoms of the disease appear, the addicted person begins to drink to avoid psychic pain.

Deterioration

Alcoholism gets worse over time. Sometimes the drinking behavior plateaus; it remains constant for months or even years. Without intervention and treatment, however, the course of the disease moves toward greater and more serious physical, mental, and spiritual deterioration.

To arrest alcoholism permanently, addicted people have to seek help. In the past, many thought that alcoholic men and women could not be treated effectively until they had lost everything and "hit bottom." People who care about the addicted person can precipitate a "high" bottom by creating a crisis sufficient to force the chemically dependent individual to seek help; early intervention and treatment also have a greater chance of success.

When people drink for relief rather than for pleasure, and consume alcohol as a drug, not a beverage, they are in trouble with the chemical. Their behavior may also deteriorate. Some addicted people sneak drinks. Having a few drinks before going out in the evening, one man insures enough alcohol in his bloodstream in case there is no opportunity to have more later. An alcoholic woman religious tends bar at community parties and "freshens" her cocktail every time she makes one for another member.

Both of these addicted persons convince themselves that others do not understand their need for a drink or they judge the other partygoers to be uptight, unable to relax and have a good time. Eventually, they deny, rationalize, and project blame for their actions.

Behind these defenses, alcoholic men and women's guilt about drinking increases while their self-worth erodes.

Loss Of Control

E.M. Jellinek identifies loss of control as the critical step into alcoholism's *addictive* phase: a person can no longer have "just one"; any drinking of alcohol starts a chain reaction experienced by the addicted individual as a physical demand for the chemical. Addicted people can still decide whether to begin drinking, but once started they are unable to predict consistently how long they will go on drinking or how much they will consume.

Some alcoholic men and women try to stop drinking on their own. Many become "dry drunks": temporarily abstinent, but still tense, nervous, easily frustrated, and anxious and preoccupied consciously or unconsciously with thoughts of drinking or not drinking. These men and women have stopped consuming alcohol but they have failed to start working on their spiritual, emotional, and physical recovery.

Some current accounts of alcoholism give less importance to cravings, compulsions, and the loss of control often cited previously as features of the disease. These reports mention that alcoholic men and women who relapse cite anger, frustration, resentment, and social temptations as the trigger for their drinking and not a need for the drug welling up automatically within them. A problem in controlling alcohol use, however, is certainly one of the signs of the disease.

Some Of The Defenses: Blame, Denial, Rationalization, And Minimization

By the time alcoholic men and women lose control, other people are worried about their drinking. Addicted people can be depressed, listless, and complain of undefined fears, sleep difficulties and a loss of appetite. The chronic and unpredictable anger of some alienates others. Personal appearance and health frequently deteriorate due to lack of proper exercise and nutrition. Some family and community members and co-workers express concern; others become angry and threaten the alcoholic person.

In the face of such pressure many addicted persons become more defensive. They deny their addiction, evade questions, blame others for their difficulties, and make excuses for their actions. In time, the defense system of alcoholic men and women becomes so highly developed that they cannot see what is obvious to everyone else: their behavior and the defense they use to explain it away are bizzare.

Behind this behavior, chemically dependent persons are ashamed about their inability to stay sober. Their neglect of others causes them guilt; their loss of friends, hurt and loneliness; the possible loss of job and alcohol supply, fear.

Most people in the addicted man or woman's life, however, are privy to few of these feelings. Instead, they listen to an increasing number of rationalizations, are frustrated by the chemically dependent man or woman's projection of blame, and worry about the addicted person's grandiose delusions.

For example, one addicted man often pointed to the previous evening's dinner as the source of his early morning headache and nausea. A woman religious complained to her community that she was forced to find her support in alcohol because of their lack of concern. Still another priest deflected his community's pressure about his addiction, boasting that the diocesan office quickly got into a mess when he failed to show up for work for a few days. He failed to mention, however, that his chemical abuse was the cause of his absence. Many of the rationalizations that alcoholic men and women use to convince others and themselves that they do not have a disease are symptoms of the disease itself.

Eventually, a combination of physiological dependence and psychological defensiveness controls the deteriorating behavior of addicted people. A number of them begin to protect their supply, making sure alcohol is always available to them and putting more and more money into the drug. Some experience mood swings and personality changes while drinking. They become temperamental, hyperactive, or vacillate between elation and sadness. For some, these changes are very obvious; for others, quite subtle. Increasingly egocentric, a number of alcoholic men and women indulge in extravagant self-pity and take unreasonable offense at the slightest provocation.

Friends, exasperated with failed attempts to stop the drinking of some chemically dependent people, begin to avoid them and stop extending social invitations, putting distance between themselves and the addicted man or woman.

Family and community life and work-performance and ministry can also deteriorate. For example, as a dependent person continues to drink to excess, families often become more isolated and cut off from social events; a religious community may restrict its drinking to certain times and places or lock the liquor cabinet. Family or community members close ranks for mutual support and survival, cutting off the addicted person.

The "Morning Drink" And Withdrawal

When a chemically dependent person experiences withdrawal symptoms, physical addiction is complete. What are the most common symptoms? A tremor in the hand, tongue or eyelids, headache, dry mouth, nausea, weakness, sweating, depression, and irritability. For some alcoholic men and women convulsions, hallucinations, and delusions may also accompany their attempts to stop drinking. Delirium tremens (the D.T.s), one of the most dramatic symptoms, is also one of the rarest, affecting only about five percent of alcoholic persons who suffer withdrawal.

About this time, some chemically dependent persons look for a "morning drink." Awakening early in the morning, their body craves alcohol. Even with the loss of control, a number of them have been able to restrict their drinking to certain times of the day. Now they need a drink in the morning to quell withdrawal symptoms and help them face the hours ahead. Eventually drinks at lunch and other intervals throughout the day are added to the morning drink and some addicted persons experience their first prolonged intoxication lasting several days.

For those so affected these "benders" mark the onset of alcoholism's *chronic* stage. Conventional wisdom maintains that the addicted man or woman in this stage has lost friends, job, and self-respect. While some chronically alcoholic people fit this description, many do not. For example, some priests, sisters, and brothers lose neither job nor much time from work, and their fellow priests or community members attempt to adjust to their disease. A few continue in responsible leadership positions in their ministries, dioceses, and religious congregations.

As the addicted person's disease progresses, however, colleagues and family and community members feel its effects. In time, some can become as sick as the addict. Among this number are enablers, men and women who protect alcoholic persons from the consequences of their addiction.

Enablers

Enablers forestall the crises that could give addicted men and women and their families and communities the chance for change. As the disease progresses, they step in more frequently to save the dependent person from pain. Some insist that alcohol is not the problem: if his employer were more appreciative or her friends more understanding, the dependent man or woman would not drink so much. Although they threaten, cajole, and exact promises, their actions permit the alcoholic person to continue drinking.

Enablers act out of a sincere but misguided sense of loyalty. Shame and fear motivate them: they hope to protect the family or group's reputation and self-respect.

Alcohol counselor Ruth Maxwell points out that many enablers are misguided by these two principles: they attempt to control the addicted person's drinking; and they find and try to eliminate this individual's reasons for drinking. As a consequence, they avoid concentrating on the alcoholic person's *need for treatment*, and the enabler's *responsibility to make his or her own life manageable*. The recovery process for enablers can

only begin when they realize that they never had any
control over the alcoholic person's drinking.

Enabling, like alcoholism, starts imperceptibly.
When the dependent person's social drinking ends
more often in intoxication, enablers begin to make
excuses and smooth over embarrassing situations. For
example, when Susan gets drunk at a party and knocks
over a tray of glasses, her husband Jack apologizes and
mumbles about Susan's pressures at work. A provincial
offers a "geographical cure" to a teaching brother
whose alcoholism includes a morning drink. By giving
the brother a new assignment and community, the
superior helps the man rationalize that he will do better in a larger school and new living situation.

Enablers get serious about their role when they
assume the addicted person's responsibilities. If a religious brother's pattern of drinking throughout the
evenings and weekends leaves him unable to do the
chores at home, enabling community members take
over the housekeeping tasks the entire group had
agreed to divide equally. A co-worker completes the
unfinished work of a hospital administrator, because
this woman's drinking interferes with her work responsibilities. As chemically dependent men and women become more irresponsible, enablers compensate
by taking over for them.

Enablers pay a price for their role. Their fear and
rage go unexpressed and they lose hope eventually of
managing those feelings with satisfaction. Enabling
spouses worry a great deal; some are plagued with
these questions: "What if he doesn't take care of the
children while I'm out at work?" "What if she doesn't

come home?" "What if he spends all his pay on liquor?" In rectories and religious communities, enablers ask similar questions: "What if he drives home drunk from the game?" "What if he fails to show up to celebrate the early morning mass?" "What if she is drunk at the school meeting?"

Many enablers misuse faith and religion: they pray for miracles instead of taking steps to change their lives. Some enabling priests and men and women religious cite charity as their reason for excusing the inappropriate behavior of their alcoholic fellow ministers or for completing their undone work. This rationale is a misunderstanding of the virtue and allows addicted sisters, priests, and brothers to avoid the consequences of their drinking.

With all the difficulties they face, why do enablers continue their efforts? Chiefly to avoid pain. Alcoholic men and women and their family members deny their shame: the fear that in some essential way they have failed as human beings.

Shame, the feeling of being exposed as helpless and worthless, is at the base of all addictions. It develops when the interpersonal bridge between two people is damaged and their relationship is called suddenly into question. John and Linda Friel describe the dynamic of shame induction in this way: imagine that you are surrounded by all of the people you love. You are in the center; they encircle you. Each and everyone of them is pointing a finger at you and, with eyes glaring, saying, "Shame, shame, shame on you! You are bad! You are stupid! You are ugly! You are clumsy!" When ashamed, people feel ostracized, cut

off from the human race. Rather than helping a
person say, "I made a mistake," shame leads an individual to believe, "I am a mistake."

To recover, enablers need to make several
changes. First, they must look squarely at their own
helplessness and admit this fact: *no one can make another
person stop drinking.*

Next, they need to *stop running from the disease and
learn the facts about alcoholism.* They have to realize that
the alcoholic man or woman will not recover without
outside assistance. Instead of hiding their search for
help, recovering enablers need to tell the addicted
person and family or religious community about the
steps they are taking.

They also need to *avoid threatening, cajoling, preach-
ing, and lecturing* and, instead, start saying what they
feel and doing what they say. If this change means
facing the chemically dependent person with inappropriate actions and behavior, they do so.

For example, if a fellow priest damages the community car while driving intoxicated, the recovering
enabler confronts the alcoholic person with his responsibility, states the facts in a loving way, and suggests the need for treatment.

Finally, enablers must *concentrate on their own
actions and get help themselves.* Al-Anon, a worldwide
self-help organization, includes many spouses,
families, parents, friends, fellow priests, and religious
brothers and sisters of alcoholic men and women. Its
members are united by this common bond: their lives
have been deeply affected by another person's drinking. By attending regular meetings, reading Al-Anon

literature, and daily practicing Twelve Step Living, members learn to grow spiritually and begin their own recovery.

Once enablers start their recovery process, what will the alcoholic man or woman do? Some do nothing; they continue drinking and die. Others, however, make changes. Alcoholism can only exist in an atmosphere that tacitly accepts the disease.

When family members stop making efforts to change the alcoholic man or woman and, instead, change themselves, the dependent person is confronted continually with his or her behavior. A pressure builds up eventually inside the addicted man or woman that can be a force to change his or her behavior. When chemically dependent persons cannot count on the help of family or community members, when their guilt goes unrelieved because spouses and children will not fight with them, when family and community members refuse to get them out of trouble — then, and often then only, will addicted men and women be forced to face up to things. As enablers change, chemically dependent persons have to become abstinent or seek out new people and situations that condone their drinking.

Summary

Once it develops, alcoholism is a chronic disorder. Vaillant points out that its course can be insidious, fulminating or intermittent. The disease is also primary, progressive, and, left untreated, always fatal.

Chemical dependency that goes untreated can kill you; the disease of alcoholism has put an end to the lives of a number of addicted men and women.

Alcoholism is also a family disease: each member feels its effects. In the next two chapters we will examine the impact of chemical abuse on families and communities living with an alcoholic member and describe the rules and roles they assume in an attempt to cope.

REFERENCES FOR CHAPTER I

Barney, Conrad. *Time is All We Have: Four Weeks at the Betty Ford Center.* (New York: Arbor House, 1986).

Black, Claudia. *It Will Never Happen to Me.* (Denver, CO: Medical Administration Company, 1982).

Cermak, Timmen L. *A Time to Heal.* (Los Angeles, CA: Jeremy P. Tarcher, Inc., 1988).

Ford, Betty. *Betty: A Glad Awakening* (New York, NY: Doubleday, 1987).

Freil, John and Linda. *Adult Children: The Secrets of Dysfunctional Families.* (Deerfield Beach, FL: Health Communications, Inc., 1988).

Johnson Institute. *Alcoholism: A Treatable Disease.* (Minneapolis, MN: Johnson Institute, 1972).

Maxwell, Ruth. *The Booze Battle.* (New York: Ballantine Books, 1976).

Sammon, Sean D. "Alcohol Intervention: First Step To Recovery," *The Priest* 43 (1987): 13-19.

The Harvard Medical School Mental Health Letter Staff. "What is Alcoholism — Part I," *The Harvard Medical School Mental Health Letter* 2 (April 1986): 1-4.

The Harvard Medical School Mental Health Letter Staff. "What is
    Alcoholism — Part II," *The Harvard Medical School Mental
    Health Letter* 2 (May 1986): 1-4.
Vaillant, George E. *The Natural History of Alcoholism.* (Cambridge,
    MA: Harvard University Press, 1983).
Wegscheider, Sharon. *Another Chance: Hope and Health for the
    Alcoholic Family.* (Palo Alto, CA: Science and Behavior
    Books, 1981).
Wholey, Dennis. *The Courage to Change.* (Boston, MA: Houghton
    Mifflin Company, 1984).

REFLECTION QUESTIONS

*1. ACoAs are at high risk to develop the disease of
    alcoholism. Spend some time thinking about your own
    alcohol use. During the last three (six, or twelve) months, what
    has been your experience with alcohol, your attitudes about it
    and feelings toward it? What place does alcohol occupy in
    your life today?*

*2. Have you experienced some of the "early warning
    signs" of alcoholism? Are you preoccupied with the drug:
    do you look forward to drinking and the feelings that come
    with it? Has your tolerance for alcohol grown over the past few
    months or years? While drinking alcohol, have you ever been
    unable to recall events, conversations, promises that you
    made?*

PART II

ALCOHOLISM AND THE FAMILY

CHAPTER II

Alcoholism And The Family

Jones gets depressed every Father's Day. His father was a mean drunk, and Jones remembers his terror as a boy walking home from school and wondering what he would find when he got there. He remembers the cold knot in his stomach, the weak knees, the pounding pulse. Would his father be home drunk and ugly, terrorizing his mother? Would he have to watch his father punch his mother again today? Would the old man beat him and his brothers and sisters?

Jones, middle-aged now, remembers the fear and shame and the sense of abandonment he felt as a boy. He kept it to himself then, of course, because kids were forbidden to air a family's dirty laundry.

Jones belongs to a fellowship called Adult Children of Alcoholics where he has met hundreds of fellow sufferers scarred by growing up in alcoholic homes. They share what they call a "dirty-laundry list" of negative traits. "We're afraid of other people, especially authority figures," Jones says. "We're terrified of any display of anger. We judge ourselves harshly. Our self-esteem is low. We take ourselves too seriously. Many of us become alcoholics, marry alcoholics, or both. We confuse love with pity. We feel guilty if we stand up for ourselves instead of giving in to others. We seek approval and lose our identity in the process. We feel we're different from other people. We avoid conflict or aggravate it, but we seldom deal with it. We fear rejection, yet we reject others. We fear criticism, yet we criticize others. We're extremely loyal even when loyalty isn't warranted. We seek immediate gratification. We don't set priorities or goals. We have difficulty following through on projects. We manage our time poorly. We fear failure, yet we sabotage success."

When he looks back on his childhood years, Jones understands why he is the way he is. Sometimes his father was away from home for weeks or months; those were the happiest times in Jones' childhood. He was free. His neighbors felt sorry for him, being temporarily without a father, but Jones was sorry only because the situation wasn't permanent. He relaxed when his father was out of the house. There was laughter at the dinner table, for a change.

The only problem when his father was away was knowing he would come back. The old man always turned up eventually. Fear turned to rage in Jones as a teenager. He had been raised to obey the Commandments, to honor his father and mother, but how much abuse could he take? There was a terrible confrontation at home one night. "You hit my mother again and I'll punch you out!" he screamed at his father. His mother, crying, tried to keep them apart. "Don't fight with your father," she pleaded. But he did. He knocked his father down the stairs. Jones can still see him sprawled in the hallway, dead drunk.

"Those things leave scars," Jones says today. "All my sisters and brothers are fouled up. They're drinkers, gamblers, compulsive eaters, neurotics. But there's hope for us. By attending meetings of Adult Children of Alcoholics, we identify with each other and learn to face ourselves and our shortcomings honestly. We stop running from painful feelings. We learn to love ourselves, which frees us to love others in a new, healthy way."

Jones has found peace of mind. But he'll be glad when Father's Day is passed.

Adapted from Bill Reel's column,
"Life with father was a tragedy,"
New York Daily News, May 23, 1985.

H AVE YOU EVER WATCHED a mobile moving gently in a summer breeze? As one part moves up, another moves down to restore the figure's balance. When a piece shifts to the right, other also drift in that direction. Mobiles are delicate systems that work to maintain their balance.

Families also operate as systems. Members are linked together for a common purpose; rules govern their life and interaction. As systems, families adjust to maintain their balance. When money is short, members cut back on spending and budget expenses; the group works together to solve its financial problems.

What about addicted families? They have trouble keeping balance; their attempts at stability are always flawed. The results of several studies point out the dysfunction in these families: greater risk of divorce, child abuse, marital strife, separation.

Alcohol counselor Sharon Wegscheider's comparison of children from alcoholic homes with those from other troubled families produced these statistics: three times as many children from addicted families are placed in foster homes, twice as many marry under the age of sixteen, the incidence of juvenile delinquency is much higher, twice the number develop emotional illness, the number of suicides is greater.

Family members who adjust to chemical dependency suffer consequences. Most CoAs avoid inviting friends home; some assume the care of younger brothers and sisters and the undone housekeeping chores of their alcoholic parents. Many skip childhood; unable to relax, they become adults before having the opportunity to be children.

Flawed adjustments to addiction extend beyond the family's children. The spouses of alcoholic men and women are often angry and guilt-ridden, filled with shame and self-hate. A woman waits up until her intoxicated husband arrives home so that she can move his illegally parked car. She also changes the bedsheets when he gets sick following a night of drinking. With their self-esteem assaulted constantly, many family members develop physical and emotional illness: adjusting to addiction can result in ulcers, colitis, and the abuse of chemicals.

Are all alcoholic families alike? No. The impact of the disease varies from family to family, and from individual to individual within the group. Sociologist Robert Ackerman offers three primary reasons for these differences: *(1) degree of alcoholism, (2) type of alcoholic, (3) family members' perception of life with the addicted person.*

The *degree of alcoholism* refers to the problem's severity and its effects on parenting. How frequent is the drinking? Daily, only on weekends, in binges? Is the addicted person able to hold down a job, function in social situations?

The manner in which alcoholic adults fulfill their parenting role affects children more than their drinking. Some are able to function outside the family: they work, and develop a social life but fail at being good parents. Many ACoAs still remember and resent the fact that their alcoholic parents were nice to everyone but their own family.

There are many different *types of alcoholic men and women.* Some are jovial when drinking, joke inappropriately, and fail to take themselves or other people seriously. Others are belligerent and abusive; they look for arguments. Still others are unpredictable: highly passive one day; physically, emotionally, or sexually abusive the next. Many restrict their drinking to the home, others imbibe only outside the family setting. Each type has an impact on those who live with it.

What factor is most important in determining the reaction of family members to alcoholism? *Their perception of its effects.* The damage done to CoAs often comes not from what parents do, but from how their children interpret the events happening at home. Some feel they are living within a crisis situation and are totally devastated. Other, believing the disease is not harmful to them, may be affected minimally.

A few CoAs appear to fare better than their peers. What characteristics set them apart? The ability to:

1. attract and use the support of adults;
2. master their own environment and have a sense of their own power, often volunteering to help others; '
3. develop a high degree of autonomy early in life;
4. get involved in various activities or projects and do well in most things they undertake;
5. be socially at ease and make those around them feel comfortable.

Other factors mediate alcoholism's effects on children:

birth order; number of youngsters in the family; child's age when the parent's chemical use begins;

sex of the addicted parent (children with alcoholic
mothers are more severely affected than those
with alcoholic fathers); chemical dependency in
both parents; the presence of other addictions in
the family (e.g., gambling, sex, food, etc.); avail-
ability of other nurturing adults like grand-
parents, aunts, uncles, neighbors, teachers, a
parish priest, etc.; unusual athletic or intellectual
talents in the child.

Regardless of the disease's impact, the dependent
man or woman's chemical use generally dominates
family life. Other members become enablers; they
forestall the crises that could start recovery for the
addicted person and themselves.

In time the family's identity mirrors that of the
alcoholic person. Each member becomes co-
dependent, sharing the disease and its symptoms:
guilt; shame; highly developed defenses; repressed
painful feelings; rigid and compulsive behavior; restricted communication. Eventually, the system that
should support the group supports only the disease. At
this point the family needs more than alcohol education for recovery.

Rules In An Alcoholic Family

Every family has its rules. They establish lines of
authority, communication patterns, and the group's
values, attitudes, and goals. A family's rules determine
its reaction to change.

Healthy families formulate rules with all members in mind. Their realistic, human, and flexible directives foster communication. Members can be themselves: their self-worth is validated. Stated simply, in healthy families rules affirm everyone's different needs and capabilities; each member is encouraged to change and grow.

What are some examples of a healthy family's rules? Wegscheider offers several: you may not hit anyone in the family; you are expected to leave the bathtub clean for the next person's use; you are expected to be home by midnight, or give a call; you need to take responsibility for developing a value system.

In alcoholic families rules are unrealistic, inflexible, and inhuman. Who benefits? No one. The alcoholic person maintains access to the chemical; other family members sidestep the intervention necessary for change. All try to avoid their pain but realize eventually that their rules encourage only self-deception and dishonesty with others. Despite this destructive outcome, alcoholic families persist in their use of these four unhealthy rules: denial, silence, rigidity, and isolation.

1. Denial

Men and women often use denial to protect themselves from a reality that is too painful to accept. In the face of a catastrophe, it can be a healthy defense giving people a temporary protective shield until they are able to make sense of the tragedy.

In addicted families unhealthy denial is life's cornerstone, a foundation for the basic conflict of many CoAs: the discrepancy between what they *see* happening within their family, and what they are *told* is taking place. For example, some CoAs *see* mom passed out every day when they come home from school but are *told*: "Everything is fine, and don't tell anyone mom is sick again." Others are *told*, "We are one happy family, we enjoy being together." What do they *see?* Adults belittling and fighting with one another. Stated simply, this rule is cardinal in an alcoholic family: *"There's nothing wrong here and don't you dare tell anyone."* An alcoholic family's denial begins with the denial that there is any problem with alcohol.

By age nine most CoAs learn to deny what goes on at home. To survive, they hide and ignore their feelings: fears that dad will lose his job, embarrassment when mom shows up drunk at graduation, sadness in realizing how much they dread the holidays, anger about all the broken promises, guilt that they cannot heal their family's pain.

Why do CoAs disregard and deny their feelings? Because they are unable to validate them. Some stop feeling altogether. To hide his pain, Steve, a thirteen-year-old from an addicted family, denied and minimized his feelings and family situation. When asked why others felt angry, scared, and disappointed though he did not, Steve replied, "Maybe because I have to be tough." Like other CoAs, he had learned to take care of himself.

Many CoAs guess at their emotions or read the reactions of others trying to figure out what they *should* feel. For some, only extreme feelings like rage, grief, and terror are real.

ACoAs, then, end up with an impaired sense of reality. Without help, few challenge the rule of denial as did Katherine, a character in Candace Flynt's novel, *Mother Love*. Speaking to her sisters about their deceased alcoholic mother, Katherine said, "We aren't going to rosy her up. We're going to remember her as she was. No purple haze. It's not disloyal. If we're going to spend time remembering, we should remember her for how she was. . . . If she were here, nobody would be having any fun."

Most ACoAs fail to understand what goes on in their world. Distrusting themselves and others, they live by this motto: If I imagine that it's not happening, maybe it will go away. Eventually, a number pretend that some things are just not taking place.

2. Silence

The "don't talk" rule enforces silence and secrecy. Members learn early not to "air their family's dirty laundry"; they are forbidden to discuss troubling situations with each other or people outside the family. The rule of silence also bans talk about feelings and emotions.

Addicted families don't talk about the real issues. CoAs often reach adulthood without having discussed their parent's addiction with anyone, including other family members.

Susan, woman religious and an ACoA, had a father who would drink and drive. During his daughter's childhood years, he often took her with him when he went out to bars. Although Susan enjoyed being with her father, she was terrified when he was behind the wheel intoxicated. At age eleven, Susan learned to drive by pushing her drunken father out from behind the steering wheel, and driving the car home herself. She continued this practice for several years.

Not until she was an adult did Susan tell anyone about her fear of driving with her father or that, as a child, she had to drive him home. What price did Susan pay for keeping this secret? She became extremely frightened when she was not driving; Susan felt she had to drive or something terrible would happen.

CoAs believe that talking only makes things worse. Disclosure of the family's secret will bring rejection: who would like them knowing their parents fought bitterly over mom's drinking or that dad was abusive when drunk? Talking might also get dad upset; drinking would follow with the implication the child had caused it. CoAs fail to learn this fact: nothing anyone says or does *makes* a chemically dependent person drink. *Alcoholic men and women drink because they have a disease.*

How can ACoAs get free of the rule of silence? By beginning their journey of recovery. How can they accomplish this task? By learning three things: how to recognize the addiction in their family, how to talk about what happened to them, and how to express their feelings.

3. Rigidity

Alcoholic families are inflexible. They become more and more rigid as they adjust to the chemically dependent person's unpredictable behavior. Family members pay a high price: deterioration paralleling that of the addicted man or woman. Faced with the alcoholic person's blaming and self-righteous behavior, they feel shame and hate themselves. Eventually, family members feel helpless, abused, hurt, rejected, lonely, out of control.

The alcoholic family's rigid structure stops children from growing up emotionally. Jack, a forty-year-old religious priest and ACoA, summed up his feelings this way: "I'm a grown man, but when I'm with my parents I feel as if I'm five years old. I'm afraid to speak up for myself and walk around like I'm on pins and needles." Paradoxically, although Jack responds emotionally like a child when with his parents, he also feels that he lost his childhood. The freedom and joys of those years were never his.

In adulthood, the rule of rigidity becomes a need to control. Rigid rules of behavior can control unpredictable situations. They also undermine playfulness, spontaneity, and real happiness.

4. Isolation

How do members survive in alcoholic families? Chiefly by avoidance. They isolate themselves from one another and their community. These patterns lead

to adult difficulties with trust and intimate relationships. Gerard, a 35-year-old religious brother and
ACoA, complained continually of loneliness, even
when he was in a relationship. He often felt he was
missing something that others appeared to have. "I
used to think that sex meant intimacy," he said with
frustration. "Now I know that it is more than that, but
what, I'm not sure."

The structure of the alcoholic family works
against intimacy developing; members deny feelings
and facts about behavior, fail to talk about what is
going on, lack trust, and, for survival, isolate
themselves from one another and those outside the
group.

CoAs contend with an environment characterized
by inconsistency and fear, guilt and blame, anger and
resentment, secrecy and denial. *To recover they need to
break their family rules*, a task that is neither quick nor
easy.

REFERENCES FOR CHAPTER II

Ackerman, Robert J. *Children of Alcoholics*. (Holmes Beach, FL:
    Learning Publications, Inc., 1983).

_____ *Same House, Different Homes: Why Adult Children of Alcoholics
    are not All the Same*. (Pompano Beach, FL: Health Com-
    munications, Inc., 1987).

Black, Claudia. *It Will Never Happen to Me*. (Denver, CO: Medical
    Administration Company, 1982).

Deutsch, Charles. *Children of Alcoholics*. (Pompano Beach, FL: Health Communications, Inc., 1983).

Flynt, Candace. *Mother Love*. (New York, NY: New American Library, 1987).

Kritsbery, Wayne. *The Adult Children of Alcoholics*. (Pompano Beach, FL: Health Communications, Inc., 1985).

Sammon, Sean D. "Understanding the Children of Alcoholic Parents," *Human Development* 8 (1987): 28-35.

Seixas, Judith S. and Youcha, Geraldine. *Children of Alcoholism: A Survivor's Manual*. (New York, NY: Crown Publishers, Inc., 1985).

V., Rachel. *Family Secrets: Life Stories of Adult Children of Alcoholics*. (San Francisco, CA: Harper and Row, Inc., 1987).

Wegscheider, Sharon. *Another Chance: Hope and Health for the Alcoholic Family*. (Palo Alto, CA: Science and Behavior Books, 1981).

Woititz, Janet Geringer. *Adult Children of Alcoholics*. (Pompano Beach, FL: Health Communications, Inc., 1983).

REFLECTION QUESTIONS

1. Consider the rules in your family. Were they healthy or unhealthy? Did they help or hinder your growth? Have you carried your family's rules into adulthood? If so, spend some time describing how they operate in your life today.

2. *Can you spot the rules of denial, silence, rigidity, and
    isolation in your life today? While you were growing up,
    did your family live by these rules? What makes you keep them
    as an adult? What must you do to free yourself of the unhealthy
    aspect of each of these rules:*

<ul>
<li style="list-style:none">a. *Denial:*</li>
</ul>

<ul>
<li style="list-style:none">b. *Silence:*</li>
</ul>

<ul>
<li style="list-style:none">c. *Rigidity:*</li>
</ul>

<ul>
<li style="list-style:none">d. *Isolation:*</li>
</ul>

CHAPTER III

The Roles People
Play In An Addicted Family

Sharon is tired of taking care of the needs of everyone else. This middle-aged woman religious wonders what it would be like if she treated herself as well as she does others.

Growing up in a family with an alcoholic mother, Sharon learned quickly that some things did not get done correctly or, often, at all, unless she did them. From childhood on, other family members looked to her to take charge, insure that everything went well, and bring a measure of self-respect and pride to the group. Sometimes, Sharon wondered if her decision to enter religious life was not, in part, motivated by her need to make things right in her family. After all, when she joined her community, people still considered it an honor to have a family member who was a priest, sister, or brother.

Sharon continued to be a "good girl" within the community. The fixed schedule and careful regulation of life found there provided welcome relief from the chaos of her family. She followed the rules, took on agreeably whatever tasks the community sent her way, and was seen quickly as a leader within the group. Sharon knew she had too little time for herself but felt guilty when she tried to fix this situation. She often wondered who would do the work if she did not.

In recent months, however, Sharon has felt increasingly more empty and unhappy. She also resents the demands of others. In trying to do everything "right," she becomes over-extended, frequently unable to say "no," even to unreasonable demands on her time and energy. She also feels lonely and cut off from others. Sharon knows she needs to make some changes in her life but sometimes it appears that "running away" is the only solution to her dilemma.

In almost everyone else's eyes Sharon is a "hero"; to herself, however, she is little more than a frightened and anxious woman who is always trying to please others. More and more she wonders where her life is heading.

W HAT ARE the characteristics that most ACoAs have in common? Human relations counselor Janet Geringer Woititz identifies at least a dozen: ACoAs

1) usually feel they are different from other people;

2) take themselves *very* seriously: they have difficulty letting go, relaxing, having fun;

3) judge themselves without mercy;

4) are superresponsible or superirresponsible;

5) have difficulty with intimate relationships;

6) lie when it would be just as easy to tell the truth;

7) are impulsive, often locking themselves into a course of action without giving serious consideration to alternative behaviors or possible consequences;

8) have difficulty following a project through from beginning to end;

9) are extremely loyal, even in the face of evidence that their loyalty is undeserved: they develop incredible tolerance for inappropriate behavior on the part of others;

10) constantly seek approval and affirmation;

11) overreact to changes over which they have no control;

12) guess at what is normal.

Where are these characteristics evident? In the roles that family members take up as they adjust to the disease in their midst.

Roles In An Addicted Family

During times of stress family members often assume roles to deal with the crisis at hand. When the tension subsides, they shed these patterns of behavior. At the death of a family member, for example, someone becomes the group's "organizer" and attends to necessary funeral arrangements. Other members are then free to experience their grief more fully. In terms of roles, nonaddicted families delegate authority appropriately: children are not given the responsibility of parenting.

In alcoholic families, roles are fixed, rigid, and follow the children into adulthood. Aspects of two described by Wegscheider are found commonly among ACoAs who are priests and men and women religious: the hero and the lost or forgotten child; the two remaining roles, rebel and mascot, are seen less often.

Heroes

Who are the heroes in any alcoholic family? Those warm, sensitive, and likable people who take care of the needs of everyone else. They come in two types: *responsible* and *placating*.

Generosity is an attractive trait. Heroes, however, purchase it at the price of their own well-being; they can't say "no." Appearing larger than life, they find it difficult to accept this fact: to be human is to be limited. This 45-year-old woman religious ACoA gets to the heart of the matter: "I'm a compulsive giver who needs to learn to be more selfish. I must quit serving everyone else at my own expense, but I don't know how, I feel so guilty."

Responsible Heroes

Usually the family's oldest child, heroes grow up feeling special. Other children look to them for leadership; adults praise their behavior. Claudia Black points out that *responsible heroes* provide structure and consistency to alcoholic families when life is chaotic and unpredictable. If mom and dad are out drinking together, these heroes ensure that the other children complete their homework, direct them to their bedrooms, and instruct them to change into their pajamas and go to bed.

ACoA specialists Herb Gravitz and Julie Bowden provide this example of a *responsible hero.* An eight-year-old girl described her fear when awakened by a fight between her parents about her father's drinking. As the shouting grew louder and sounds of breaking glass and slapping mounted, she encouraged her younger sister to move over into her bed. Over the smaller child's sobbing, her older sister reassured her, "It's all right. Daddy won't hurt Mommy, and they'll make up. Everything will be fine, just you wait and see." The older girl set aside her own terror to parent her sister. *Responsible heroes* make life easier for parents: the addicted man or woman can be preoccupied with drinking, the spouse with the alcoholic person.

Responsible heroes also learn to be completely self-reliant. If adults are undependable, what is the best way to achieve stability? Provide for it yourself. *Responsible heroes* end up living by this motto: "If you want to get something done, do it yourself."

Feeling abandoned, many look outside the family for a sense of well-being. They fantasize about leaving home as soon as they can. Finally, *responsible heroes* excel at short-term goals. "What will I get done today?" "What can I expect to complete tomorrow?" By setting and reaching tangible goals, *responsible heroes* achieve a sense of accomplishment. These CoAs are doers; their lives are marked by action. *Placators* are another type of hero. While also active, much of their energy is channelled into rescuing others.

Placating Heroes

The *placating hero* is one of the most sensitive
children in an addicted family. These youngsters take
care of everyone else's emotional needs, making life
bearable for other family members. They comfort
brothers and sisters embarrassed by mom's drunken
behavior at the supermarket and dispel their siblings'
anger when dad breaks another promise.

Placators rarely appear very upset: they seem to
have few expectations and fail to show disappointment
when plans fall through; if troubled they keep it to
themselves. At school these apparently sensitive, un-
selfish, and uncomplaining children divert attention
from themselves and focus it on others. They are seen
as good, giving people, always nervously trying to
please. *Placators* are usually well-liked. Small wonder,
since all their efforts are spent attending to others.

All heroes try to make up for their family's weakness, correct its imbalance, heal its pain. They are the
"best little boys and girls in the world." Rather than
satisfy their own needs, they dedicate their life to an
impossible dream: making up for the family's lack of
self-worth.

In spite of the odds, heroes provide moments of
hope and pride for their family. They usually excel in
what they undertake, collect trophies, and are seen as
accomplished, successful men and women. Can they
heal their family's pain completely? No. As a result,
heroes always feel inadequate. No accomplishment is ever
enough; something more must always be done before
heroes can take pride in their achievements.

What consequences do heroes face as adults? *Responsible heroes* continue to take charge. Most assume leadership roles, seeking out organized situations where they can be in control. They find it difficult to relax. For them, life is serious business; they are awkward and uncomfortable with frivolity. By their mid-twenties most are isolated from people: heroes take care of others but rarely allow for mutual relationships. They fail to learn the rules of human relationships and instead develop a keen sense of observation. Responsible heroes find it easier to react to their world rather than interact with it.

Placating heroes are similar: "nice" people who care for the needs of others. Their relationships lack mutuality; *placators* give a great deal but take very little. As empathic listeners, they divert attention from themselves; their time is spent pleasing people, making them feel better. They are excellent negotiators, masterful at resolving conflicts. Ardent *placators* never disagree; they are the first to apologize even when an apology is unnecessary.

Placators rarely consider what *they* want; they forever discount *their* needs. Most cannot safely explore this question: "What can *you* do for *you* so that *you'll* feel better?" Consequently, they rarely get what they want from life.

How do most adult heroes feel? Empty and unhappy. They experience little sense of accomplishment. Some are lonely and depressed; others, frightened and anxious. Most wonder about life's meaning. For all, the source of their difficulties is elusive.

The Hero
In Priesthood And Religious Life

Priesthood and religious life have often attracted heroes. These life choices emphasized perfection, control, self-discipline, and disregard of personal needs. Both provided members with a ready-made identity, and the opportunity to take care of others. What fertile ground for the hero's role to flourish!

A young teenager, for example, left home for the minor seminary, and met with academic and athletic success. He appeared to get along well with his classmates. At times, this young man looked "too good to be true." Others struggled with adolescent growing pains; he seemed to have no problems.

In time, however, a perceptive observer noticed that this hero's need to achieve, to be the best, had taken on a compulsive quality. He was never satisfied with himself, always had to do more, reach greater heights. By midlife, this young hero may burn out: trying to be perfect and caring for the needs of others at the expense of his own can be destructive.

Some women religious trade the role of hero at home for that of an overly responsible community member. Overextending themselves continually, most plan to do more in an average day than could ever be done realistically; they fail to realize that a twelve-hour day is *not* a half day's work. These women, and many priests and brothers, were taught that "good" priests and religious should always be available. They never say "no," fail to set realistic limits, and keep busy and overwork. Burnout is a constant danger. Their spirituality is often shallow. While they may look like saints, their sanctity has a compulsive quality: they *have* to be good.

Many heroes in religious life and priesthood, especially those who establish a life independent of their family, also suffer "survivor guilt." Psychiatrist Tim Cermak points out that for some, it takes the form of depression. What is the source of this guilt? Violation of an unspoken rule in addicted families: no one can get any healthier than the sickest member. Having established an independent life, many heroes fear their success is a sign of callousness toward family members still entangled in the disease. Consequently, some heroes in priesthood and religious life are pulled back to their family; they try once again to "fix" things.

Heroes And Alcohol

What about heroes and alcohol? Some begin adult life as confirmed abstainers. Many others do not. The drug performs wonders for them: it makes them less rigid, looser, more relaxed. They feel adequate and assertive; talk more freely about themselves; express anger. A few even allow themselves to be selfish.

Many heroes turn to alcohol when they get tired of giving so much of themselves to others. The drug helps them escape; it gives them some relief from the constant demands other people place on their time and energy. With these results, one drink can lead to a second, a third, and a fourth. By midlife some heroes are in trouble with alcohol.

Lost Or Forgotten Children

Who feel most like outsiders in an addicted family? Forgotten children. They are literally lost about their place within the group. Usually middle children, these boys and girls are born into an emotionally overloaded situation. To the relief of its other members, they accept their unimportance, retire to the fringes of the family, make few demands. Most end up feeling sad, confused, and fearful.

Lost children are "invisible" children; they have an overwhelming sense of personal inadequacy. Most withdraw into a fantasy world: imaginary friends become their companions. Here they are safe, secure, in control.

At school, these youngsters rarely speak up. Their written works may be done well, but they agonize when called upon to speak out in front of others. Frequently, they feign illness to avoid school and other potentially stressful situations.

Most forgotten children get lost in the shuffle. Consequently, their social development is stunted. Unable to express their feelings, they have no way to make their needs known to others. Lost children have little experience in living; fail to learn the skills needed for relationships; make errors in judgment. The emotional life of other people remains a mystery to them.

Many have a difficult time during adolescence: they are overwhelmed by their burgeoning sexuality and pressure to be part of their peer culture. To survive they withdraw and take pleasure in solitary activities: eating, watching TV, listening to music.

How do lost children fare as adults? Many hide out; they carry their low self-worth into adulthood. Others become self-reliant and independent. Still others take whatever happens in stride: they avoid making waves. The stunted social growth of all, however, leads to trouble with intimacy. Most lost children believe that their chances for satisfying love relationships are slim. Without a doubt, *loneliness* is their most characteristic feeling. Eating remains a gratification for many: they eat compulsively to fill up their emotional emptiness. Others compensate through materialism, placing great value on possessions and pleasure.

Do lost children have a sense of life direction? Claudia Black doubts it. Having been ignored for so long, most feel powerless with little sense of choice. Many adopt the attitudes and values of others to compensate for the lack of their own; most fail to make their own decisions, and, instead, look to authority for direction. Does this situation make them angry? No. Instead, it leaves lost children feeling helpless, lonely, and worthless. A 35-year-old woman religious put it succinctly: "I feel as if I've been on a roller coaster for a long, long time."

Chemical dependency counsellor Marie Schutt identifies two types of adult lost children: *passive manipulators, passive acceptors.*

1. *Passive manipulators* are guilt-inducing martyrs living lives of quiet resignation. They appear proper and morally correct, and helpless and clinging, but are quite skilled at controlling most situations through

passive manipulation. Their faults are difficult to define.

Passive manipulators doubt their ability to make decisions: their lives are full of fear and indecision. Most appear to value the opinions of others more than their own. However, they also maneuver others into making the decisions they want made. To what advantage? If the decision turns out to be the wrong one, the passive manipulator is free of responsibility.

One ACoA described her lost child mother this way: "She was small and delicate, but had a will of iron. She never yelled; all she had to do was look. I would just feel so full of guilt I couldn't stand it. I don't remember a time when I didn't think I had to take care of her."

2. *Passive acceptors* believe in magic. They have a child-like faith in the future and believe that circumstances will change without any action on their part. What is the passive acceptor's motto? Things will change.

Most passive acceptors live in a They feel unimportant and believe they are unable to control any aspect of their destiny. Having failed to learn direct communication with others, they are unable to express their needs, wants, and dreams to those with whom they live and work. They are always worried about hurting the feelings of others or disappointing them. Most passive acceptors put up with their lot in life; many continue to live in intolerable situations long after hope is gone.

Lost Children
In Priesthood And Religious Life

At one time, the Church, and religious and priestly life offered a safe haven to some lost children. Here they found a place in life and an answer to their questions about identity, life direction, sexuality, and peer relationships. Obscurity was considered virtuous, relationships were carefully regulated, and the lost child's love of solitude and rich inner world could pass as a spiritual personality. Many became invisible in the diocese and community, out of sight and mind: the group's loner. The sisterhood, brotherhood, and priesthood often allowed this survivor of the alcoholic family to take a back seat in life.

Many forgotten children in Church service spent their growing up years praying for a miracle: that somehow God would put a stop to their parent's drinking. When these prayers went unanswered, they looked to religious life and priesthood for a place of security and the opportunity to make up for what was lacking in life and family.

A number of priests, sisters, and brothers who are lost children have the potential to develop a deep spirituality. Their solitude, love of quiet, and rich fantasy life offer some ingredients for spiritual growth and can become the building blocks of their recovery. However, without a capacity for mature intimacy, the spirituality of these men and women will become little more than an escape.

Forgotten Children And Alcohol

What about lost children and alcohol? The drug often gives them a false sense of power: it temporarily removes their feeling of helplessness. With this newfound strength comes increased self-confidence. Although they often suffer from eating disorders, lost children also run the risk of becoming psychologically addicted to alcohol: it provides access to feelings they do not experience normally.

What, then, are common characteristics of ACoA lost children? Wegscheider identifies a half dozen: low profile; self-reliance; eating disorders; confusion about sex roles and sometimes sexual identity; feelings of helplessness, loneliness, and worthlessness; taking inordinate comfort and pride in possessions. Lost children need help to build a solid sense of self-worth.

Rebels

Rebels use anger as an effective survival tool and carry this unrealistic attitude throughout life: hostility, rudeness, and physical intimidation will usually get you what you want.

Often the child born second, rebels arrive in a family where the addicted person consumes everyone's attention and energy, a heavy load burdens the enabler, and the hero has captured the spotlight. Very little room is left for this newcomer.

Rebels would rather be heroes but have to look for another role. Virtue and talent notwithstanding, they cannot compete: heroes are usually older, bigger, and firmly entrenched.

Most rebels have a strained relationship with heroes; they feel inferior and come eventually to envy them. This unrealistic thinking develops into a troubling animosity: nothing the hero does is any good. In time, he or she resents the rebel's constant criticism.

Rebels look to external sources for the cause of their anger. When they find life unrewarding, they fail to see that their behavior helped create this situation. They also have difficulties with authority: rebels criticize and condemn anyone whom they believe wants them to change or conform; their sense of justice is attuned to peers and underdogs.

Like all CoAs, rebels desperately need their parent's attention and approval. Children develop self-worth when treated in ways that demonstrate their value and importance. The rebel's erratic behavior, however, invites angry retaliation, not acceptance; most fail to develop consistent feelings of self-worth. If the truth be told, rebels do not really approve of themselves.

Rebels come to expect little affection or understanding from their family. Acting like the hero fails to bring satisfaction; belligerence invites angry retaliation. After a while, rebels withdraw and spend more and more time away from home. Seeking out peers who provide support and companionship, they are attracted to youngsters who act out their frustrations. These friends accept the rebel uncritically, as long as his or her behavior conforms to their values. Even-

tually, most rebels find self-worth only with their
friends; the peer group becomes increasingly
important.

As they mature, a number of rebels experiment
with sex and drugs, and their exploits often shock their
family. Searching for intimacy, many become sexually
involved at an early age. However, they fail to find the
deep, caring, and mutually satisfying relationships
they seek. A number become chemically dependent;
they use drugs to escape the harsh realities of their life.
Those who do not develop an addiction often marry
someone who does. This relationship allows them to
continue being angry and chronically dissatisfied.

Rebels feel lonely and unhappy. They possess
poor social skills and are self-centered, shallow, man-
ipulative, and exploitative. A number are real suicide
risks.

Rebels
In Priesthood And Religious Life

Rebels who fail to work at their own recovery are
underrepresented in religious life and priesthood.
What reasons account for this situation? First of all,
during their early years of formation these men and
women are usually angry, chronically dissatisfied, and
in constant conflict with authority. Second, their
presence is a tremendous tension within the community; some control others through verbal abuse or physical force. These CoAs end up having too much difficulty with formation and usually withdraw from the
seminary or novitiate.

The lives of some rebels, however, are changed forever through a relationship with a priest, sister, or brother. Their defenses are challenged by the religious man or woman's concern, honesty, and compassion; rebels begin to realize that they do not have to violate their value system to win the acceptance of others. Eventually, the recovery process gets underway; they accept the role alcohol played in their family's life and its influence on their own.

The journey of recovery is neither swift nor easy. Many rebels withdraw initially and send this clear message: do not waste your time with me. What challenge faces adults in their work with rebels? Help them separate from their family and realize their own self-worth.

Some recovering rebels are represented among the ranks of priests, sisters, and brothers. These caring and compassionate adults often demonstrate an uncanny ability to reach young people on whom others have given up. Perhaps their gift is an ability to see something of themselves in these troubled young rebels.

Rebels And Alcohol

Rebels usually develop alcohol dependency at an earlier age than other CoAs. For many, it is a central part of the life of their peer group. Alcohol gives rebels a false sense of confidence; it makes them feel better about themselves. Early intervention and treatment leading to recovery are essential.

Mascots

How do mascots reduce tension in addicted families? By clowning around. They use humor to divert attention from the group's alcohol dependency. Who is the mascot in most chemically dependent families? The youngest child.

Even healthy families "baby" last borns: they protect them from life's harsh realities. Alcoholic families go a step further and hide important facts from their youngest.

The mascot's problem has its roots in this fact: family members withhold information and report things that are untrue. Something in the group is terribly wrong, the mascot knows it, everyone else hides the fact. The results are devastating: many mascots fear losing their mind; they learn to mistrust their experience. A diocesan priest recalled that during childhood he often lay awake listening to his parents argue bitterly about his mother's alcoholism. These battles lasted well into the night and left him wondering if his family would survive intact. When morning came, however, and others in the house gathered around the breakfast table, everyone acted as if the night before had been quiet and uneventful. The boy began to wonder about his sanity.

Family therapist Virginia Satir calls mascots "distractors." They are master manipulators. Their task is clear: distract in order to diffuse. While still toddlers, these children learn that showing off brings rewards: everyone laughs; the addicted person and family crisis escape the spotlight; the distractor is in control and gets some attention. Mascots resort to clowning every time life presents a difficult situation; their humor diffuses the tension. For a short period, family members can avoid dealing with their feelings of inadequacy, unimportance, shame, guilt, and loneliness.

Tense, anxious, and overactive, many mascots are diagnosed incorrectly as hyperkinetic by school authorities. A number also run the risk of remaining children forever. Because their self-worth is shaky, they use avoidance and distraction to deal with difficult challenges and questions. Other adults dismiss them as jokers. Their relationships end up shallow and flighty.

Mascots never learn to deal with stress. Their families are overprotective and mascots learn eventually to overprotect themselves. Fear is their most characteristic feeling. Who among ACoAs have the greatest risk for developing emotional problems? Mascots. Psychiatric illness and suicide are common among these adult children.

Mascots
In Priesthood And Religious Life

Some mascots find their place in religious and priestly life. Dioceses and congregations have all known jokers, incessant talkers, people with annoying distracting mannerisms, or fragile members whom the group protects. Are all of them mascots? No. The behavior of those who are, however, helps distract the

group; it can avoid dealing with difficulties that arise.
Mascots do for their fellow priests, brothers, and sisters
what they did for their families: shift the spotlight away
from problems, reduce the group's tension.

Mascots And Alcoholism

What about mascots and addiction? Pain is a powerful motivator for change; mascots use drugs to avoid
both. While still youngsters, some use mood-altering
substances to help them deal with the day-to-day pressure of life. They learn quickly this fact of life: chemicals can dull pain and quiet chronic fears.

Do mascots have characteristic features? Yes.
Wegscheider identifies seven: immaturity, apparent
fragility, hyperactivity, clowning, overdressing, super-
sexiness, or other bids to attract attention.

Summary

Children of alcoholics often take up roles in their
struggle for survival. Some ACoAs fit rather easily into
the description of the hero, rebel, lost child, or mascot;
others do not. They find a mix of traits within
themselves.

Whether or not the role descriptions fit neatly, all
ACoAs need to be concerned about their recovery.
Chapter IV examines this challenge.

REFERENCES FOR CHAPTER III

Black, Claudia. *It Will Never Happen to Me.* (Denver, CO: Medical Administration Company, 1982).

Cermak, Timmen L. *A Time to Heal.* (Los Angeles, CA: Jeremy P. Tarcher, Inc., 1988).

Gravitz, Herbert L. and Bowden, Julie D. *Guide to Recovery.* (Holmes Beach, FL: Learning Publications, Inc., 1985).

Sammon, Sean D. "Understanding the Children of Alcoholic Parents," *Human Development* 8 (1987): 28-35.

Satir, Virginia. *Peoplemaking.* (Palo Alto, CA: Science and Behavior Books, 1973).

Schutt, Marie. *Wives of Alcoholics.* (Pompano Beach, FL: Health Communications, Inc., 1985).

Woititz, Janet Geringer. *Adult Children of Alcoholics.* (Pompano Beach, FL: Health Communications, Inc., 1983).

Wegscheider, Sharon. *Another Chance: Hope and Health for the Alcoholic Family.* (Palo Alto, CA: Science and Behavior Books, 1981).

REFLECTION QUESTIONS

1.   Are you a hero? A lost child? Maybe you see in yourself the traits of a mascot or rebel. Or perhaps, like many ACoAs, you identify with the characteristics of several roles. Spend time thinking about how CoA roles apply to you and your family members.

2. *Have you carried the traits of a hero, rebel, lost child, or mascot into your adult years? Where do you see them manifested? Do they interfere with your happiness, your relationships, your self-esteem? If so, in what ways?*

3. *Many people find some ACoA traits attractive: heroes are generous, mascots amuse, and lost children don't clamor for attention. What positive ACoA traits attract you? What feelings are behind these attractive qualities?*

4. *Does the thought of giving up some of your CoA traits frighten you? If so, of what are you afraid?*

PART III

RECOVERY

CHAPTER IV

The Process Of Recovery

"This article reads as though it were written just for me," thought Julie excitedly. "You would think its author had been a member of my family." This 35-year-old woman religious had picked up the evening newspaper and in her reading come across an article entitled "Alcohol and the Family."

Julie had grown up in a family where her father's alcohol use was a problem. From childhood on she believed that everyone else's family was happy while hers was a mess! She carried with her feelings of shame about her father's drinking, her family, and herself.

Why was the article such a revelation to Julie? She saw in herself many of the characteristics of adult children of alcoholics: the need to be in control of everyone and everything; workaholism; overresponsibility; low self-esteem; a fear of being close to others.

The recovery model developed by Herb Gravitz, Julie Bowden, and Tim Cermak is summarized in this chapter. Readers seeking more detailed descriptions of the process should refer to: Herbert L. Gravitz and Julie Bowden's *Guide to Recovery* (Holmes Beach, FL: Learning Publications, Inc., 1985) and Timmen L. Cermak's *A Time for Healing* (Los Angeles, CA: Jeremy P. Tarcher, Inc., 1988).

The article's author also wrote about the process of recovery and described group meetings for people from alcoholic homes. "I'm not a group person," thought Julie. "Anyway, what good will it do to drag up all those things that happened in the past. Isn't it better to 'let sleeping dogs lie'?"

The description of people involved in the recovery process was so seductive, however, that Julie found it hard to dismiss the article. "Perhaps I can change," she thought. "Maybe I don't have to spend the rest of my life with shame and painful feelings. Maybe there is some help for me also." Julie was not sure about what to do next. She was certain about only one thing: the thought of recovery was exciting and frightening at the same time.

DESPITE widespread recognition of alcoholism as a family disease, ACoAs continue to be ignored, misdiagnosed, and treated inappropriately. Traditional mental health approaches are insufficient for adult children because they fail to recognize and treat the specificity of their condition. ACoAs have a common bond: a recognizable, diagnosable, and treatable condition. They deserve understanding, information, and help to break free from their isolation and silence.

Today, recovery for adult children is within reach; it begins when ACoAs are willing to make the past real. They foster the healing process by making contacts with their inner child and validating what that child felt while growing up. As recovery gets underway, the ACoA's past is reclaimed and integrated into the present. How is this task accomplished? By examining wounds that alcoholic families inflict on growing children and the potentially dangerous ways ACoAs have developed to care for these wounds. Painful past events can never be changed; their pain, however, need not be carried into the present.

Is the journey of recovery different for adult children who are priests, sisters, and brothers than for other ACoAs? Not really. For each person, it begins with this first step: acknowledgment of the family's addiction.

Therapists Tim Cermak, Herb Gravitz, and Julie Bowden identify six predictable stages in the recovery process: *survival, reidentification, core issues, integration, tranformations,* and *genesis*. While some of these stages are painful, adult children need to avoid skipping any.

Above all else, ACoAs should remember this fact about recovery: *it takes time.* The process moves at the adult child's pace; it is gradual, incremental, and often imperceptible.

What do ACoAs have to watch for as they undertake recovery? Anything that can interfere with the process:

(1) their own addiction to alcohol, drugs, sex, food, etc.;

(2) magical thinking about recovery: the belief that it is something people "catch," like a cold;

(3) attempts to do it alone;

(4) approaching the process as an intellectual exercise, failing to see it also as a task of heart and spirit.

1. Survival

Recovery begins with the survival of childhood. How do most ACoAs arrive at this stage? By keeping family rules and carrying fixed and rigid roles into adulthood. As we have seen, adult children are experts at dodging and hiding, and negotiating and adapting, just to stay alive. This strategy exacts a price. Boundaries between feelings, thoughts, behaviors get blurred: love is confused with caretaking, spontaneity with irrationality, intimacy with sex, and anger with violence.

Lessons learned in childhood tend to endure. CoAs reach maturity feeling damaged; their shame is intense; many of their personality characteristics stem from childhood strategies for coping with chaos and catastrophe. Growing up in an addicted family creates wounds that go underground and most ACoAs react to current situations as if living still in their childhood home. The loss of trust in oneself and the world, along with losses of spontaneity and the ability to relax, are wounds that can last for a lifetime.

Many ACoA priests, brothers, and sisters get stuck in the survival stage; they experience a sourceless discomfort. Some refuse to examine their feelings about a parent's alcoholism; others deny it altogether; still others insist they are not like their alcoholic parents: they choose to remain unaware of how much the family's addiction affected them and other family members.

A number of adult children also have a problem with identity. They face this task: *label accurately who and what you are so that you can discern the real sources of pain in your life.* Without a diagnosis of the problem, no healing is possible. The first step toward recovery is to acknowledge the family's addiction.

Intimacy is especially troublesome during the survival stage. Most adult children trust completely or not at all; they fail to find a middle ground. Some overwhelm strangers with an onslaught of openness. Others become obsessed with a relationship and feel empty and frightened when it is over. Still others, fearful of self-disclosure, conclude that people get hurt by caring too much. Do the relationships of ACoAs follow a predictable pattern? Yes. They often sour and come to an end.

During the survival stage, many adult children search for something to lessen their pain. Some put their energies into self-improvement, attending assertiveness or self-esteem workshops; others turn to compulsive eating, shopping, gambling, drug and alcohol use, or sexual behavior. All are wary of trust, warmth and caring, freedom and choice, and give-and-take. To enter recovery's second stage, some intervention is necessary.

2. Reidentification

A newspaper article about adult children, attendance at a conference addressing addiction and the family, or a television interview discussing the topic can initiate the stage of reidentification.

Why should people identify as ACoAs? First of all, to surrender the shroud of secrecy and shame that is the hallmark of an addicted family. Next, to become aware of genetic, physical, emotional, and spiritual vulnerabilities acquired growing up in an alcoholic home. Finally, such identification provides a framework upon which to construct a realistic view of the past. Many adult children begin to acknowledge their childhood environment for what it was: a war zone. The conflict might have been a "cold" or "hot" war, but it was war, nonetheless.

A subtle difference exists between the adult child's admission of parental alcoholism and his or her self-identification as an ACoA. The first places attention outside oneself; the second, inside. Recovery's second stage brings with it a variety of feelings: hope about the future; anger at having lost one's childhood; guilt. Some ACoAs worry: have the family and its secret been betrayed? No. The ACoA has simply stopped colluding with the group about its alcoholism.

Adult children cannot force recovery's reidentification stage. Some try to push themselves through feelings of rage, loss, and abandonment, hoping to gain control over them, and reverse the past. Healing cannot take place according to a controlled time frame. *ACoAs need to experience their feelings because it is important to do so and for no other reason.* They must surrender their control in order to heal.

a. *Twelve Step Living.* Adult children also need to recover through the Twelve Steps of Alcoholics Anonymous. Al-Anon and ACoA groups are central to this process. They help adult children learn what it has been like for others who have been close to an addicted person. More importantly, group participation breaks down feelings of isolation and shame; the ACoA realizes: "I am not alone." However, all Al-Anon and ACoA meetings are not the same. Some adult children are dissatisfied following their first contact with the group. Attend at least a half dozen meetings with different groups before drawing any conclusions.

What are the Twelve Steps? We:

1. Admitted we were powerless over the effects of alcoholism — that our lives had become unmanageable.

2. Came to believe that a Power greater than ourselves could restore us to sanity.

3. Made a decision to turn our will and our lives over to the care of God as we understood Him.

4. Made a searching inventory of ourselves.

5. Admitted to God, to ourselves, and to another human being the exact nature of our wrongs.

6. Were ready to have God remove all these defects of character.

7. Humbly asked Him to remove our shortcomings.

8. Made a list of all persons we had harmed, and became willing to make amends to them all.

9. Made direct amends to such people wherever possible, except when to do so would injure them or others.

10. Continued to take personal inventory and when we were wrong promptly admitted it.

11. Sought through prayer and meditation to improve our conscious contact with God as we understood Him, praying only for knowledge of His will for us and the power to carry that out.

12. Having had a spiritual awakening as the result of these steps, we tried to carry this message to alcoholics, and to practice these principles in all our affairs.

How do A.A.'s Twelve Steps apply to adult children? In a number of ways. Denial ends when people confront the facts about their life. To start the process of recovery ACoAs must accept the reality of their parent's alcoholism. The first of the Twelve Steps helps them to take on this identity: "adult child of an alcoholic." Honest acceptance of the label opens channels of healing that were blocked previously.

A.A.'s second and third steps call on adult children to rely for healing on a Power other than themselves. These steps require some faith. Communion with God, however you conceive of the Higher Power, reopens feelings of belonging and being at home with oneself.

Steps four and five help ACoAs to be honest with themselves. They are asked to write down a thorough inventory of their weaknesses *and* strengths, past and present, and to share this list with another person.

The next two steps free ACoAs from their pettiness and resentments, self-pity and an all-too-ready

Grateful acknowledgment is made for permission to print the Twelve Steps of Alcoholics Anonymous, copyright 1939, A.A. World Services, Inc. All rights reserved. The interpretation of the Twelve Steps included in the present text, however, is not the opinion of A.A. World Services, Inc.

willingness to neglect the spiritual core of their recovery.

Steps eight and nine follow. What do they teach adult children? That honesty and their own integrity are more important than the impressions others have about them. Taken together these two steps are a powerful part of the process of healing.

Finally, ten, eleven, and twelve are maintenance steps. They put spirituality where it belongs: at the core of healing. To recover, adult children need to make a commitment to the spiritual disciplines that will build a relationship with their Higher Power and to spread the good news of healing to others in need.

Twelve Traditions also guide Al-Anon and ACoA groups (see Appendix B); they provide for safety and unity and keep all self-help meetings one in form and aim.

ACoAs who refuse to investigate self-help meetings will be unsuccessful in reidentification and the later stages of recovery. Their refusal to take advantage of one of the most beneficial forms of help available today is evidence of this problem: their overwhelming need to be in control of their own recovery.

b. *Other helpful resources for recovery during the reidentification stage.* What are other helpful resources to be used during recovery's second stage? Workshops, lectures, and reading materials that teach about ACoAs, alcoholism, and co-dependency, education about alcoholism and its effects on the family. Can therapy be helpful? Yes, but only if the counsellor is knowledgeable about alcoholism and adult children. What about therapists who are also ACoAs? Be sure

they have begun their own healing process. When
searching for a counsellor, adult children need to
"shop around."

Some religious sisters who are ACoAs report that
women's groups are an important part of their recovery process. Coed groups force some women into taking nurturing roles: men do most of the talking, women most of the listening. In a women's group, however, participants cannot sit back; others ask: What
about *you*? How does this topic affect *you*? What do *you*
feel about it? Some topics like sexual abuse and incest
are also discussed more easily in a women's group. The
setting allows a number of women greater freedom to
express their anger about these violations.

Today, there are also a growing number of
residential treatment programs for ACoAs. The
shorter ones last from five to eight days; the longer
programs, about four weeks. The best residential treatment is always connected to ongoing therapy. In this
way, the gains realized in an intensive program can be
carried over into life after residency.

Many adult children ask: is it necessary to deal
with parents and family during the reidentification
stage? Gravitz and Bowden advise approaching them
slowly, thoughtfully, and with caution, if at all. ACoAs
have spent a lifetime as caretakers; they naturally assume responsibility for others. At this stage and
throughout their recovery, adult children need to care
for themselves, not parents and family.

Recovery's second stage is painful; facing the past
and its effects is not an easy task. With the acknowledgment of parental alcoholism, forgotten and

painful memories often bubble up. They help ACoAs make sense of their adult years in light of childhood experiences. As reidentification moves forward, adult children begin to recognize their core issues, the results of growing up in an addicted family. Recovery's next stage is about to get underway.

3. Core Issues

Psychiatrist Tim Cermak identifies several characteristics that touch the lives of nearly every ACoA: control (the compulsive need to be in charge of everything and everyone); workaholism, a preoccupation with projects and things that just "have to be done"; mistrust; defensiveness; a fear of being close to others; chronic anger; a constant sense of being ignored, attacked, misunderstood; martyr identity or long suffering; avoidance of feelings; a chronic sense of emptiness; overresponsibility; a constant search for rules and guidelines to bring happiness and social and emotional success; ignoring one's personal needs; an inability to separate from family.

To these Julie Bowden and Herb Gravitz add a number of others: all-or-none functioning (things are either all right or all wrong, seldom in between); extremely low self-esteem; and emotional anesthesia (a dissociation between events and feelings). Having been raised in a chaotic environment, many adult children are also "adrenaline junkies." They thrive on crises and emergencies; when life is stable and uneventful they become depressed and anxious.

Certain events consistently trigger an ACoA's core issues: intimate relationships, life transitions, unexpected happenings, family visits, and the evaluation of one's performance. Faced with these situations, most adult children fall back on familiar behavior patterns: increased anxiety, denial, emotional shutdown, a flurry of activity. As these strategies become increasingly ineffective, ACoAs struggle to learn new and healthy ways to cope.

What tasks face adult children during the third stage of recovery? Identify core issues; take some action. For ACoAs to slow down, explore their problems without making judgments, and develop more patience, a change in attitude is essential. How can this come about? By seeing life in new ways, and filling the gaps in learning. During the core issues stage, adult children begin to reach out and ask for help. Support groups and, at times, individual therapy are critical to this stage of recovery.

Action is a central aspect of the core issue stage. ACoAs begin to allow themselves to have needs, experiment with being spontaneous, take chances, and cease being motivated by guilt and responsibility for others. During this stage adult children also learn to form honest relationships; they stop trying to control the feelings and impressions of others.

How can ACoAs spot trouble during recovery's third stage? By being on the lookout for a half dozen warning signs:

(1) isolation, the lack of friends or family with whom to talk;

(2) excessive criticism of oneself and others;
(3) strong feelings of depression and anxiety or insecurity and fear;
(4) frequent insomnia;
(5) complete inability to manage what is being learned, experienced, or seen about oneself or one's history.
(6) most important, excessive consumption of alcohol or other drugs.

Adult children can underestimate the pervasive, insidious effects of alcoholism and the depth of the issues they face. Some minimize addiction's fallout; others are overwhelmed by hopelessness; still others berate themselves about the slow progress of their recovery. All need to guard against losing heart. By identifying their core issues and seeking help, ACoAs discover new strengths; eventually they welcome the process of change.

4. Transformations

What is the building block of an adult child's journey to recovery? Change. It transforms characteristics used to survive childhood and suitably applies them to the circumstances of adult life. What is required for the success of this effort? Time, attention, and energy. During recovery's fourth stage, ACoAs connect their past with the present; they put what they are learning into practice.

How do adult children know that transformation is underway? When they start calling things by their right names. Change begins with recognition and acceptance. In embracing their core issues, ACoAs find new ways to describe, understand, and alter some current behaviors. Prior to this stage, for example, most adult children want to regulate, legislate, direct, and supervise their own and everyone else's behavior. As youngsters, their survival depended on it. This need to control frequently masquerades as hypervigilance, anxiety, perfectionism, and unrelenting motivation.

With change, ACoAs identify this compulsive need to be in charge of everyone and everything for what it is: a problem. They also look for ways to let go of it. First of all, they realize that control is not an "all-or-none" proposition: totally manipulating self, others, and the environment versus complete resignation, going along with whatever happens.

Second, adult children learn that while some things and people can be controlled, others cannot. In time, the meaning of A.A.'s *Serenity Prayer* becomes apparent: "God, grant me the serenity to accept the things I cannot change, the courage to change the things I can, and the wisdom to know the difference."

Is dramatic change seen during this stage of recovery? Not necessarily. Transformation is often as simple as experimenting with one new behavior. Over time, however, recovering ACoAs risk feeling emotions, confiding in others, trusting at least one other person. Above all, they learn patience. What is their reward? Eventually, they can see and rejoice in their progress. Recovery's fourth stage begins to restore meaning and happiness to their life.

5. *Integration*

How do adult children know they are at the stage of integration? Their thoughts, feelings, and behaviors come together. No longer is one thing thought, another felt, and a third done. Their problems have not disappeared; they simply handle them more effectively. A feeling of calmness and joy is the reward.

Integration is linked to self-acceptance. ACoAs no longer feel compelled to get rid of adult child qualities. Instead, they realize that these characteristics helped them survive the stresses of childhood. During integration, ACoAs come to understand that these survival skills do not imprison them; they can use them or not, depending on their current needs. Used properly, many adult child traits become assets.

When ACoAs stop being victims, recovery's central therapeutic issue confronts them: care of self. Taking up this challenge leads to qualitative life changes:

(1) playing and having fun free of guilt;
(2) limit setting;
(3) intolerance of mistreatment; the thoughtless behavior of others is no longer accepted;
(4) development of appropriate trust, openness to feelings, ability to make short and long term commitments.

Tim Cermak fashions these changes into a seventeen item *Personal Bill of Rights*:

1. Life should have choices beyond mere survival.

2. I have a right to say no to anything when I do not feel ready or when it's unsafe.
3. Life should not be motivated by fear.
4. I have a right to all my feelings.
5. I am probably *not* guilty.
6. I have a right to make mistakes.
7. There is no need to smile when I cry.
8. I have a right to terminate conversations with people who make me feel diminished and humiliated.
9. I can be healthier than those around me.
10. It's okay for me to be relaxed, playful, and frivolous.
11. I have a right to change and grow.
12. It is important to set limits and to take care of myself.
13. I can be angry with someone I love.
14. I can take care of myself, no matter what circumstances I am in.
15. I do not have to be fully healed to be fully worthwhile.
16. I do not have to be perfect to be perfectly happy.
17. I do not have to be perfect, period, *no one else is.*

Grateful acknowledgment is made for permission to reprint the Personal Bill of Rights from *A Time to Heal*, copyright 1988 by Timmen T. Cermak (Los Angeles, CA: Jeremy P. Tarcher, Inc., 1988). Permission to reprint given by St. Martin's Press.

How do adult children live out these changes? By reaching out to others, giving themselves permission to make mistakes, exercising, following a healthy diet, playing and enjoying life, listening to themselves. Some decide to "grow up." One middle-aged woman religious, having long been a "good daughter" to avoid upsetting her alcoholic parents, stopped participating in family get-togethers that ended in a drunken scene. She decided finally to stop being a child.

Integration is a critical stage of recovery. ACoAs have lost touch with important parts of themselves: their thoughts, feelings, behavior — all live in separate worlds. The process of integration brings together these elements; adult children are now free to build a more complete identity.

By this point, ACoAs have begun to realize that they are their primary resource for recovery. However, many others continue to be available: friends, Al-Anon and ACoA groups, counsellors and therapists, organizations like the National Association for Children of Alcoholics (N.A.C.O.A.),* workshops, written materials, and others mentioned earlier. Throughout their recovery, adult children should use all that are helpful.

Many recovering ACoAs in priesthood and religious life worry about becoming selfish. Having ignored their own needs for so long, they feel guilty and uncomfortable whenever they put themselves first. Rather than slip back into old patterns of self-neglect, they need to check the reality of their perceptions. How? By asking trusted friends, fellow priests, sisters, and brothers for input and evaluating what is said.

Eventually, adult children learn to distinguish between selfishness and healthy self-respect. They can state their own needs and emotions clearly, allowing others to react to them as they wish. They have moved from being adult children to simply being adults.

6. Genesis

What is Genesis? A new beginning, a re-creation. This spiritual awakening most often develops over time and fills adult children with gratitude.

The Genesis stage is different for each person but involves generally a new openness to the spiritual aspects of life. It cannot be willed or forced into a timetable. Neither should it be used as a way to avoid learning to care for oneself. Instead, through commitment to the work of recovery, ACoAs become aware eventually of the spiritual connection that binds us all. Genesis is a commitment to a power beyond oneself and the visible world. Is it the same as organized religion or theology? No. Genesis speaks to universal spiritual concerns. Spirituality goes well beyond the intellect; it involves our emotions as well.

The Genesis stage emerges only after adult children have learned the meaning of surrender. Having spent their life, thus far, surviving on their own, many ACoAs are surprised to learn that the world is a more benevolent place than they imagined: it is safe to let go and allow God to be active in their life. These men and women begin to participate realistically in the creation of their world: they act rather than react; they learn what is legitimately under their control and what is not.

Men and women who follow the Twelve Steps of Alcoholics Anonymous and Al-Anon walk a spiritual path. Their recovery comes about through fellowship, working the program, and the help of a Higher Power. Like them, ACoAs need to promote actively their spiritual development. They cannot take this journey for granted, but must work at it every day.

What are some ways to accomplish this task? Reflective living, meditation, prayer. These practices can be cultivated through centering exercises, reading, the discipline of regular spiritual direction, and providing time daily for meditation and prayer.

What about parents and family during recovery's final stage? This is the time to forgive, to surrender old burdens. Not to do so isolates ACoAs through judgment and self-righteousness; forgiveness unifies and heals.

Once adult children have made the decision to forgive, the difficult part is over. Do ACoAs need to tell their parents directly? Not necessarily. Some do; others, fearing parents will not understand, choose not to; still others are unable to. Regardless of what is decided, one thing is important: adult children need to forgive parents and family members, dead or alive, wherever they may be, and wish them well.

Recovery Pitfalls
For The Hero, Lost Child, Rebel, And Mascot

The journey of recovery is not easy and each member of an alcoholic family needs to be on the lookout for pitfalls. Heroes are often the most resistant to intervention and treatment. Why? Because their role has brought them positive results along with pain. What happens when heroes surrender their role? They lose a special and honored place in the family. Heroes also have to be ready for other people's anger and disappointment as they begin to set realistic limits and start to say "no."

Lost children may fear that recovery will rob them of the time alone and solitude they have come to value. Also, some are frightened about their lack of social skills; others worry they will lose the security they have found in religion and Church.

Rebels have little else but their pain to lose in recovery. However, the burden of hurt, shame, and guilt they carry can interfere with the process of healing.

Mascots fear losing the role of clown. At least it gets them some attention! Other people have come to expect them to be performers; recovery gives them the opportunity to shed this role and their anxiety.

Summary

While one out of eight Americans is the child of an alcoholic, each can live a richer and more rewarding life by embracing Twelve Step Living.

Recovery for ACoAs is fivefold: spiritual, physical, intellectual, emotional, and volitional. It unfolds gradually. Family rules are broken; rigid childhood roles shed. Adult children learn to care for themselves;

reach out to others; find new ways of living and acting. Their decision to choose recovery is an act of faith, a spiritual commitment. They risk exploring an unknown territory, their inner self.

Some ACoAs, however, contend with another problem: their own addiction to alcohol. What additional help exists for them or any person dependent on alcohol? In Chapter V we will look at the process of intervention. A first step on the road to recovery from addiction, intervention can halt the alcoholic man or woman's spiral of deterioration and move the individual along the path to sobriety. It is one of the best tools in the fight against the disease of alcoholism.

REFERENCES FOR CHAPTER IV

Brown, Stephanie. *Treating Adult Children of Alcoholics.* (New York, NY: John Wiley and Sons, Inc., 1988).

Callahan, C.S.C., Rachel and McDonnell, S.S.N.D., Rea. *Hope for Healing: Good News for Adult Children of Alcoholics.* (Mahwah, NJ: Paulist Press, 1987).

Cermak, Timmen L. *A Time to Heal.* (Los Angeles, CA: Jeremy P. Tarcher, Inc., 1988).

---

* Additional information about the National Association for Children of Alcoholics can be obtained by writing: N.A.C.O.A., 31706 Coast Highway, Suite 201, South Laguna, CA 92677, or calling (714) 499-3889. ACoAs can also obtain more information about Alcoholics Anonymous by writing to Alcoholics Anonymous World Services, Inc., 468 Park Avenue South, New York, NY 10016 or calling (212) 686-1100. Details about Al-Anon are available from Al-Anon/Alateen Family Group Headquarters, 1372 Broadway (at 38th Street), 7th Floor, New York, NY 10018 or by calling (800) 245-4656; in New York City (212) 302-7240.

Ford, Betty. *Betty: A Glad Awakening* (New York, NY: Doubleday, 1987).

Gravitz, Herbert L. and Bowden, Julie D. *Guide to Recovery.* (Holmes Beach, FL: Learning Publications, Inc., 1985).

Kritsberg, Wayne. *The Adult Children of Alcoholics.* (Pompano Beach, FL: Health Communications, Inc., 1985).

Seixas, Judith S. and Youcha, Geraldine. *Children of Alcoholism: A Survivor's Manual.* (New York, NY: Crown Publishers, Inc., 1985).

Wegscheider, Sharon. *Another Chance: Hope and Health for the Alcoholic Family.* (Palo Alto, CA: Science and Behavior Books, Inc., 1981).

REFLECTION QUESTIONS

1. Recovery cannot be rushed. Where are you in this process and what has your journey been like? Have you experienced disappointments? Rewards? During the next several months, what steps do you need to take to continue your recovery?

2. Identify obstacles to your recovery. Do you attend Al-Anon or ACoA meetings? If not, what stops you? Do you put time aside each day to meditate? If not, what stops you? Do you work to set realistic limits? If not, what stops you? Spend some time thinking about roadblocks in your healing process.

3. *Do you believe spirituality is the core of recovery? If so, how does this belief get lived out in your day to day life?*

4. *Spend some time reflecting on the meaning of the Serenity Prayer: God, grant me the serenity to accept the things I cannot change, the courage to change the things I can, and the wisdom to know the difference.*

CHAPTER V

Intervention

When did Greg's community admit finally that they had to talk with him about his alcohol use? When the police charged him with "driving while intoxicated."

Several of Greg's fellow priests had mentioned to him previously their concern about his drinking, but his community had never sat down together as a group, expressed their alarm, and asked him to get help. A few had, in the past, insisted that there was not enough evidence to ask Greg to get some treatment. He never missed work in the parish, they pointed out. Of course, there were those few occasions when Greg was hungover and failed to get up to celebrate his assigned early morning Mass. The parishioners never knew, however, because one of Greg's fellow priests donned vestments quickly and filled in for him.

Every time a friend or colleague talked with him about his drinking or an episode involving alcohol, Greg would deny the problem or minimize what had happened. Jack thought Greg drank less after he spoke with him, but Larry assured him that Greg cut down only when Jack was around.

> *Several members of Greg's community were also amazed that he reacted to his arrest with anger, insisting there was no problem and that the arresting officer was mistaken. Obviously, something had to be done before Greg killed himself or someone else. As they talked among themselves, however, the members of Greg's community were unsure about what steps to take. Should they call their provincial and ask him to do something about Greg's drinking? Would it be better for each of them to sit down individually with Greg and express their concern? Was their upcoming community meeting the best setting in which to speak with him? How should the members of Greg's community deal with their anxiety about confronting him? What could they do if he got angry, walked out of the meeting, or refused to get treatment? Each of them knew something had to be done; just what, however, was unclear.*

WHAT IS AN INTERVENTION? A planned confrontation with an alcoholic person carried out by the significant people in the individual's life. They are armed with factual, non-judgmental data about the person's drinking and its consequences. Interveners offer specific treatment possibilities; they are also clear about what steps they will take should the dependent person refuse to seek help.

Intervention uses the evidence at hand to get the alcoholic man or woman into treatment. It creates the crisis that must happen for the addicted person to seek assistance. Chemically dependent men and women need to be presented with enough factual data to show a clear and causal relationship between alcohol use and their present dilemma. At the same time, family or community members are made aware of their co-participation in the disease.

When is there enough reason to intervene? Chemical dependency expert David Meagher answers this troublesome question in a simple and straightforward manner. He suggests you ask yourself these questions: 1) Is the person's use of alcohol causing problems in: work or school; family or community finances; the user's health; emotional stability; social setting; with the law; family or community gatherings; 2) Following a drinking episode by the person about whom you are concerned, have you ever felt: embarrassed or afraid of what others might think; scared; upset or angry; if you were a better spouse/parent/friend/community member, it would not have occurred; confused about what you can do, and 3) Have there been: family or community disagreements caused by alcohol use; promises to quit or control drinking; attempts by family or community to control the member's alcohol use? Meagher suggests that an affirmative answer to more than three of these items is good enough reason to intervene.

The Right Attitude Is Important

An attitude of loving concern on the part of people significant to the alcoholic man or woman is an essential part of any intervention. *Before attempting one, examine your own attitudes.* The addicted person has a disease, is seriously ill, and suffers from impaired judgment and a denial of reality. Regardless of the crisis that triggers the intervention, the confrontation needs to be non-punitive and non-judgmental.

If you intend to intervene, plan carefully. Some families, dioceses, religious communities, and ministry and work teams seek the assistance of an alcohol family systems counsellor when preparing to meet with the addicted person.

Regardless of the resources available, this five step formula can help with the task of intervention: *recognition, documentation, action, referral,* and *reintegration.*

Major Symptoms

First, *recognize* that a problem exists and do not turn your back on it. If you do, it will only get worse. Next, draft a list of potential intervention participants and contact each of them. Remember, let them take responsibility for saying "yes" or "no" about participating. Because of the need for clear, specific, and factual examples when confronting the alcoholic man or woman, it is important that a number of those living and, where appropriate, working with the dependent person participate in the intervention. The alcoholic man or woman's defense system is too highly developed to be breached by one person alone.

Alcohol counsellor Bill Thompson points out that some addicted men and women can be persuaded to enter treatment by suggesting that they go and discover for themselves whether or not they qualify for a diagnosis of addiction. *If persuasion if insufficient, those intervening must take a firm and decisive approach.*

When presenting the problem to the alcoholic person, it is important to describe the difficulties as you see them. *Do not evaluate.* Stated simply, do not diagnose; you are not expected to be an alcohol expert. *Documentation* comes in handy as you prepare for an intervention with the addicted man or woman. It helps to keep an accurate, up-to-date description of the chemically dependent person's behavior.

In moving into the *action* stage family and/or community members and, where appropriate, co-workers need to have a clear idea of what they will say and what unexpected situations they may encounter. The evidence presented should be factual and drink-related. Do not moralize, and avoid opinions and generalities.

The following examples of factual data were used in several interventions:

> "Marie, I've always enjoyed living in community with you but during the past two years I've been concerned about your drinking. I spoke with you a few times about this topic and on each occasion you assured me that everything was under control. At the party last week, though, you had been drinking and smelled of alcohol. You bumped into a lamp and broke it. When you apologized to our host your words were slurred. I was embarrassed for you and for myself."

> "Jeff, while we are not close friends, I've always respected and liked you. Tim spoke to me after our community meeting last night and told me how troubled he is about your drinking. He's concerned about what is happening to you and so am I. I'm afraid we are losing you and I want you to get some help."

> "Bob, one of the reasons I married you was because of your love of kids. The players on the Little League team look up to you; they appreciate the time and attention you give them. Not many fathers in this neighbor-

hood take your interest in the well-being of our young people. However, when you came in from the ball game last week, you were so drunk that your speech was slurred and your gait unsteady. When I realized you had driven home in that condition I was terrified."

"Jane, I remember when we first got married I looked forward to when we both got home from work. We'd sit and talk and tell each other how much our time together meant. Sometimes it's still like that: you listen and I feel you care. But I'm very concerned about your drinking. I know we have talked about it before but we always seem to end up fighting. Last night I found another bottle hidden in the basement laundry hamper and this discovery made me angry. I want you whole and healthy; I want you to get help."

"Steve, you've always been a good worker. In recent months, though, something has been happening to you. You often seem tired at work; you've lost your interest. The last few times we have been out to lunch to celebrate I noticed that you seem to be drinking more. This past week when we got back to the office after the birthday celebration for Jess, you had had so much to drink that you couldn't stay awake at your desk. I told you to go home. More and more I feel as though I'm covering for you."

Some interveners use descriptions of the alcoholic man or woman's conversations and appearance while intoxicated to undercut the individual's denial.

It helps to write down one's intervention statement and read it at the time of the confrontation. This process will guard against the possibility of backing away at the last minute or sanitizing one's remarks. It will also help to keep the focus on non-judgmental and non-punitive comments.

In making a list to be used during an intervention, people can draw examples from several areas: have there been changes in the person's pattern of alcohol use, his or her personality or health? Has he or she experienced legal problems, a disruption in personal activities, or created difficulties during special occasions such as holidays, graduations, and anniversaries?

An intervention should take place when the addicted man or woman is sober. The defenses of addicted people are particularly vulnerable when they are depressed and remorseful on days after a particularly bad drinking episode. An intervention "dress rehearsal" is also helpful; it allows participants the opportunity to talk about their feelings and hear aloud what they and everyone else will say.

During an intervention, participants let the dependent person know of their concern about what the disease is doing to the individual. They want the person to get any needed assistance and they are prepared to help find it.

Because of the impaired thinking and unconscious denial which result from their illness, many alcoholic men and women cannot respond to an intervention. A number may insist that they can quit or handle the problem on their own. Some suffer from a disorder called euphoric recall. In this condition, addicted men and women think they are having fun and acting properly while everyone else sees their behavior as grossly inappropriate. Blackouts and the repression of the memory of some alcohol-induced behaviors add to the individual's denial of the disease. Even a well-planned intervention, then, may not meet with success. Sometimes a religious leader is left with no choice but to order a community member into a treatment program.

Critical Step

What happens if the intervention is unsuccessful and the addicted person refuses to go into treatment but gives a solemn promise never to drink again?

In this situation use the "what if" clause. Ask, "What if you drink?" "Then certainly I'll enter treatment," would be the expected response. If it is, ask for the promise in writing.

Abstinence is only the first step on the road to sobriety. Without treatment the great majority of chemically dependent men and women will start drinking again. When that happens, the alcoholic person's written promise will send the individual into treatment.

The fourth or *referral* step is a critical one. *Addicted men and women need to recover through the Twelve Steps of Alcoholics Anonymous.* In working at this program daily, they learn to accept their disease, and come to realize that their lives have become unmanageable, and that they are powerless over their alcoholism.

As they become willing to admit their character defects and defensiveness, their attitudes change. Eventually, addicted persons come to believe in the spirituality of the program — there is a solution other than themselves: a Higher Power.

Factors To Consider

Alcoholic men and women can also benefit from some additional treatments: individual and group out-patient therapy with trained addiction specialists, and short or long term inpatient alcohol programs.

Alcohol professionals can help in choosing the most appropriate type of treatment for the addicted person. Several factors need to be considered: age; physical, mental, and spiritual health; the individual's drinking and drug-use history; and any legal problems.

Finally, as part of treatment, plans need to be made to *reintegrate* recovering alcoholic men and women into their families and communities and work and ministries. This process will vary depending on the individual and type of treatment received. Many residential programs, for example, require family members or diocesan or congregational authorities and community members to become involved in the re-entry and after-care phases of treatment. This involvement helps the reintegration process.

A well-designed inpatient chemical addiction program usually has a carefully constructed after-care program that initiates the process of reintegration well before the client's discharge from residential treatment.

Summary

Thoughtful educational programs about the disease of alcoholism need to be part of the initial and ongoing formation efforts of dioceses and religious orders and congregations, our schools' curriculum, and parish adult education programs.

Those men and women already afflicted with the disease of alcoholism do not need our despair but a redoubling of our efforts to intervene. Thus, we can offer family members, co-workers, and fellow priests, brothers, and sisters genuine assistance on their first step to recovery.

REFERENCES FOR CHAPTER V

Bratton, Mary. *A Guide to Family Intervention.* (Pompano Beach, FL: Health Communications, Inc., 1987).

Meagher, M. David. *Beginning of a Miracle.* (Pompano Beach, FL: Health Communications, Inc., 1987).

Sammon, Sean D. "Alcohol Intervention: First Step to Recovery," *The Priest* 43 (1987): 13-19.

REFLECTION QUESTIONS

1. *Is there someone in your life whose use of alcohol concerns you and other people? If so, have you ever spoken about your concern with this person? If not, what stops you? Fear? Concern about the person's anger? Violence? Your own alcohol use? Spend some time planning an intervention for the person: how do you feel about such an undertaking, who would you include, what would you say? What fears do you have about being part of the intervention?*

CONCLUSION

Until recently, the plight of CoAs went largely unnoticed. This failure was not due to ill-will but rather ignorance about the disease of alcoholism. Today, knowledge and the tools for recovery are available.

Priests, sisters, and brothers have a two-fold educational responsibility about the topic of addiction. In the first place, knowledge about alcoholism and its effects on the family helps priests, and men and women religious from chemically dependent families to increase self-understanding, reduce self-deception, and begin recovery.

What about sisters, brothers, and priests from families untouched by addiction? Alcohol education enhances their understanding of the disease and its impact, and the adult children in their midst.

Whether ACoA or not, all Church ministers have a responsibility for addiction self-education for a second important reason: the next generation. A significant number of today's children live in families with an actively alcoholic parent; they are the ACoAs of the future. Priests and men and women religious are often in close contact with these youngsters. Armed with the knowledge that early intervention enhances the chance of recovery, they can make a difference in the life of a child and family.

Alcoholism disables and kills; ACoAs who remain in the survival stage lead troubled lives. Religious leaders should encourage their priests, sisters, and brothers to give one another the respect of intervening in the life of a community member or fellow minister with an addiction problem; ACoAs deserve the same respect.

Efforts on behalf of any of alcoholism's children are richly rewarded: genuine spiritual living is the core of recovery. If you are an ACoA, begin the journey of healing; its fruits are well worth your efforts. If you know any adult children, help them take their first steps toward recovery. Your efforts will enrich their life as well as your own.

APPENDIX A

The Michigan Alcoholism Screening Test

1. Do you feel you are a normal drinker?
2. Have you ever awakened in the morning after some drinking the night before and found that you could not remember part of the evening?
3. Does your wife, husband or parents (community members, fellow priests, those who minister with you) ever worry or complain about your drinking?
4. Can you stop drinking without a struggle after one or two drinks?
5. Do you ever feel badly about your drinking?
6. Do you ever try to limit your drinking to certain times of the day or to certain places?
7. Do your friends or relatives (fellow priests or members of your community) think that you are a normal drinker?
8. Are you always able to stop when you want to?
9. Have you ever attended a meeting of Alcoholics Anonymous?
10. Have you gotten into fights when drinking?
11. Has drinking ever created problems with you and your wife (husband, fellow priests or community members)?

12. Has your wife (husband, other family members, fellow priests, or community members) ever gone to anyone for help about your drinking?
13. Have you ever lost friends or girlfriends/boyfriends because of your drinking?
14. Have you ever gotten into trouble at work because of your drinking?
15. Have you ever lost a job because of drinking?
16. Have you ever neglected your obligations, your family or work for two days or more in a row because of your drinking?
17. Do you ever drink before noon?
18. Have you ever been told you have liver trouble?
19. Have you ever had the D.T.s (delirium tremens), severe shaking, heard voices or seen things that weren't there after heavy drinking?
20. Have you ever gone to anyone for help about your drinking?
21. Have you ever been in a hospital because of your drinking?
22. Have you ever been a patient in a psychiatric hospital or on a psychiatric ward of a general hospital where drinking was part of the problem?
23. Have you ever been seen at a psychiatric or mental health clinic, or gone to a doctor or clergyman for help with an emotional problem in which drinking played a part?
24. Have you ever been arrested, even for a few hours, because of drunken behavior?
25. Have you ever been arrested for drunken driving or driving after drinking?

Scoring: 0 - 2 "yes" responses: social drinking.
            3 - 4 "yes" responses: heavy drinking.
            5 - 6 "yes" responses: alcoholism.

Reprinted by permission, from the *American Journal of Psychiatry*, Vol. 127, pp. 89-94, 1971. Copyright 1971 by the American Psychiatric Association.

APPENDIX B

The Twelve Traditions of A.A.

1. Our common welfare should come first: personal recovery depends upon A.A. unity.
2. For our group purpose there is but one ultimate authority — a loving God as He may express Himself in our group conscience. Our leaders are but trusted servants; they do not govern.
3. The only requirement for A.A. members is a desire to stop drinking.
4. Each group should be autonomous except in matters affecting other groups or A.A. as a whole.
5. Each group has but one primary purpose — to carry its message to the alcoholic who still suffers.
6. An A.A. group ought never endorse, finance, or lend the A.A. name to any related facility or outside enterprise, lest problems of money, property and prestige divert us from our primary purpose.
7. Every A.A. group ought to be fully self-supporting, declining outside contributions.
8. Alcoholics Anonymous should remain forever nonprofessional, but our service centers may employ special workers.
9. A.A., as such, ought never be organized; but we may create service boards or committees directly responsible to those they serve.

10. Alcoholics Anonymous has no opinion on outside issues; hence the A.A. name ought never be drawn into public controversy.
11. Our public relations policy is based on attraction rather than promotion; we need always maintain personal anonymity at the level of press, radio, and films.
12. Anonymity is the spiritual foundation of all our traditions, ever reminding us to place principles before personalities.

The Twelve Traditions of Al-Anon

1. Our common welfare should come first; personal progress for the greatest number depends on unity.
2. For our group purpose there is but one authority — a loving God as He may express Himself in our group conscience. Our leaders are but trusted servants; they do not govern.
3. The relatives of alcoholics, when gathered together for mutual aid, may call themselves an Al-Anon Family Group, provided that, as a group, they have no other affiliation. The only requirement for membership is that there be a problem of alcoholism in a relative or friend.
4. Each group should be autonomous, except in matters affecting another group of Al-Anon or A.A. as a whole.
5. Each Al-Anon Family Group has but one purpose: to help families of alcoholics. We do this by practicing the Twelve Steps of A.A. *ourselves*, by encouraging and understanding our alcoholic relatives, and by welcoming and giving comfort to families of alcoholics.
6. Our Al-Anon Family Groups ought never endorse, finance, or lend our name to any outside enterprise, lest problems of money, property, and prestige divert us from our primary spiritual aim. Although a separate entity, we should always cooperate with Alcoholics Anonymous.
7. Every group ought to be fully self-supporting, declining outside contributions.

8. Al-Anon Twelfth Step work should remain forever nonprofessional, but our service centers may employ special workers.

9. Our groups, as such, ought never to be organized; but we may create service boards or committees directly responsible to those they serve.

10. The Al-Anon Family Groups have no opinion on outside issues; hence our name ought never to be drawn into public controversy.

11. Our public relations policy is based on attraction rather than promotion; we need always maintain personal autonomy at the level of press, radio, T.V., and films. We need guard with special care the anonymity of all A.A. members.

12. Anonymity is the spiritual foundation of all our Traditions, ever reminding us to place principles above personalities.

The Twelve Traditions reprinted and adapted with permission of Alcoholics Anonymous World Service, Inc.

Grateful acknowledgment is made for permission to print the Twelve Traditions of Al-Anon, copyright 1973, from *One Day at a Time in Al-Anon*, by Al-Anon Family Group Headquarters, Inc. All rights reserved.

An Interesting Thought

The publication you have just finished reading is part of the apostolic efforts of the Society of St. Paul of the American Province. The Society of St. Paul is an international religious community located in 23 countries, whose particular call and ministry is to bring the message of Christ to all people through the communications media.

Following in the footsteps of their patron, St. Paul the Apostle, priests and brothers blend a life of prayer and technology as writers, editors, marketing directors, graphic designers, bookstore managers, pressmen, sound engineers, etc. in the various fields of the mass media, to announce the message of Jesus.

If you know a young man who might be interested in a religious vocation as a brother or priest and who shows talent and skill in the communications arts, ask him to consider our life and ministry. For more information at no cost or obligation write:

Vocation Office
2187 Victory Blvd.
Staten Island, NY 10314-6603
Telephone: (718) 698-3698